DOG BREEDING FOR PROFESSIONALS

by dr. herbert richards

Front cover:
A mother attending to her newborn puppies with an assist from her owner. Photos by Diane McCarty.

Back cover:
The stud mounting the bitch (upper photo) and stud and bitch in a tail-to-tail tie position after the stud has dismounted. Photos by Anne Roslin-Williams.

Frontis:
English Setter by Jeanne White.
Breeding photos: Anne Roslin-Williams.
General illustrative photos: Louise Van der Meid, and Mark Dulin - 12; Frasie - 153; Dr. Alexander Mehlman - 22; Debra Ruggiero - 32; Evelyn M. Shafer - 26; Sally Ann Thompson - 44, 168, 213; Three Lions - 54, 57, 112, 129, 149, 165, 180, 203, 204, 209, 215.

Interior Product Photos:
Courtesy, Safari Pet Centers, Sea Girt, New Jersey
Color Whelping Photos:
Cambrick's Frosted Icing, owned by Mrs. Doris Blakely, Wall Township, New Jersey.

ISBN 0-87666-659-4

Distributed in the U.S.A. by T.F.H. Publications, Inc., 211 West Sylvania Avenue, P.O. Box 27, Neptune City, N.J. 07753; in England by T.F.H. (Gt. Britain) Ltd., 13 Nutley Lane, Reigate, Surrey; in Canada to the book store and library trade by Clarke, Irwin & Company, Clarwin House, 791 St. Clair Avenue West, Toronto 10, Ontario; in Canada to the pet trade by Rolf C. Hagen Ltd., 3225 Sartelon Street, Montreal 382, Quebec; in Southeast Asia by Y.W. Ong, 9 Lorong 36 Geylang, Singapore 14; in Australia and the south Pacific by Pet Imports Pty. Ltd., P.O. Box 149, Brookvale 2100, N.S.W., Australia. Published by T.F.H. Publications, Inc. Ltd., The British Crown Colony of Hong Kong.

Contents

Introduction

If breeding is indeed a natural phenomenon (and we all surely will agree that it is), why should man interfere with the normal breeding instincts of his dog? Obviously one reason is to avoid untimely or unwanted pregnancies, but oftentimes we also want to selectively breed for certain desirable traits and avoid those characteristics which breeders deem undesirable. Many of the various dog breeds we enjoy today have developed only after hundreds of years of selective breeding. Most breeders want to preserve the desirable traits of a breed, and this is best done by controlling the dogs' natural breeding behavior and channeling the stud's enthusiasm towards the desired bitch.

Breeders should witness the mating act to ensure that there are no complications. For example, a bitch might turn on the stud and the ensuing quarrel could result in physical injuries. Additionally, the breeder will want to be able to testify that a successful mating occurred and involved only one stud. Most people naively believe that two dogs know just what to do if left alone—unfortunately, this is not always the case. Dogs have their preferences and you can't expect them to readily accept a stranger or undesirable mate.

Breeding dogs is like so many other endeavors in life. . . once you make a major activity of them, you not only beautifully refine and sophisticate whatever you are doing, but you also introduce more probability of "something going wrong." That is, your intensification of the activity also intensifies otherwise small problems. Hopefully this guide on breeding dogs will help you avoid—or at least correct—those things which might otherwise go awry.

This book discusses the key requirements for successfully breeding good dogs:

1. Selection of parents for desirable traits and temperament.
2. Dry, warm, clean and spacious quarters.
3. Sunlight and fresh air.
4. Balanced exercise and rest.
5. Balanced diet and regular feeding schedule.
6. Love and companionship.

Though a natural phenomenon, mating will not necessarily occur when two dogs are left to themselves. Owners will want to accustom their animals to interference with the mating process, not only to assist in the case of dogs being bred for the first time, but to guard against injury, more likely to occur to the valuable stud dog than to the bitch. Here, breeders help these Brussels Griffons to compensate for a size difference.

CHAPTER ONE

Who First Bred Dogs?

Although sheep were probably the first animals to be domesticated, Mesolithic hunting folk most likely domesticated dogs for companionship and protection, as well as for hunting partners in driving and rounding up elusive game.

Today, the only true wild dogs are the Australian dingos—wolves and coyotes are not dogs. Wolves and prehistoric wild dogs were probably first tamed for companionship and loyalty. Although primitive man was known to eat dogs (indeed, some people in foreign countries *still* eat dogs), we would like to believe that dogs were kept for companionship rather than to serve as a ready food supply.

Unlike mules (sterile hybrid offspring from a horse-donkey breeding), fox-dog hybrids and wolf-dog hybrids are often fertile. This fact alone bespeaks of a close relationship between these species that undoubtedly dates back to prehistoric times.

In his book (1791) entitled *Travels through North & South Carolina, Georgia, East & West Florida, the Cherokee country, the extensive territories of the Muscogulges or Creek Confederacy, and the country of the Chactaws; containing an account of the soil and natural productions of those regions, together with observations on the manners of the Indians—embellished with copper plates,* the traveler William Bartram reports that he saw "... a troop of horses under the control and care of a single black dog, which seemed to differ in no respect from the wolf of Florida, except his being able to bark as the common dog." So there we see the wolf again!

The broad muzzle and the great variety in size exhibited by some of the excavated remains of these ancient dogs (or dog fore-

The modern day Australian dingo represents the only true wild dog. Here a city zoo is home for this dingo mother and her young family.

runners) could have been some of the results of breeding. Middle East archeological sites, as well as northeastern European ones, reveal unmistakable evidence of dogs—bones and figurines—as early as sixty to eighty centuries before Christ.

The mysterious Mound Builders of the great serpent mound, snaking through Ohio, domesticated only dogs, as far as archeological evidence goes. Pre-Columbian Peruvians bred three distinct kinds of dogs. We could follow with example after example of the dog's long-enduring march alongside (and inside) man's development.

So there is nothing very new about the idea of breeding dogs. . . just about how best to do it. . . and that is what this book is all about.

CHAPTER TWO

Dog Anatomy and Physiology

THE STUD

The dog's copulatory organ, the penis, is composed of soft erectile tissue with a small central bone and, during erection, has a bulbous enlargement at its base. A sheath of skin (prepuce) covers the penis and the scrotum surrounds the two sperm-producing testicles. Suspending the testicles in a scrotum is nature's way of providing them with a cooler temperature than the rest of the body. This cooler temperature is apparently necessary for the production of sperm as testicles that have not descended into the scrotum do not produce sperm. Testicles that are only partially descended produce few, if any, viable sperm.

The scrotum is a pouch of skin between the thighs which is divided into two sections, each containing one testicle. A hormone secreted by the testicles (testosterone) is responsible for the development of the male dog's sex characteristics. Ducts connect the testicles with the penis. The fluid carrying the sperm cells is called the semen.

During sexual excitement the penis swells and becomes rigid; pressure on sensitive nerves behind the penis bone cause the dog to thrust. The penis penetrates a constricting muscular ring at the opening of the bitch's vagina and swells even more, thus the bulbous enlargement prevents withdrawal—this interlocking phenomeon is called a *tie.* At no time or under no circumstances should a forced separation be encouraged during this tie. During the tie the sperm-laden semen is ejaculated in spurts. In fifteen to thirty minutes after the copulatory act began, the swollen penis will return to normal size and can be withdrawn.

The sperm cells are motile with a *head*, *neck*, and motile *tail*. Their life span in the female reproductive tract is about twenty-four hours. Although sperm are continually being produced, the sperm count of an overused stud will decline. However, after a resting period the sperm count will again increase. The amount of time required for the sperm count to return to normal varies according to the breed and the individual dog. This count may be determined by microscopic examination of semen specimens and actual sperm counts.

THE BITCH

The bitch's ovaries produce the ova, or eggs, and the hormones responsible for her female sex characteristics. The ovaries are paired organs located high up behind the last ribs and just behind the kidneys. Two tiny fallopian tubes encapsulate the ovaries and connect each ovary to the upper end of each uterine horn. These arm-like extensions from the main uterine body are where the fetuses develop. This Y-shaped uterus of dogs contrasts markedly from the pear-shaped uterus of humans. The cervix, or mouth of the uterus, is tightly closed except during heat or when the bitch is whelping. The next portion of the female's reproductive tract is the vagina. The bitch's vagina terminates at the exterior portion of the tract, the vulva. The vulva is located just below the anus.

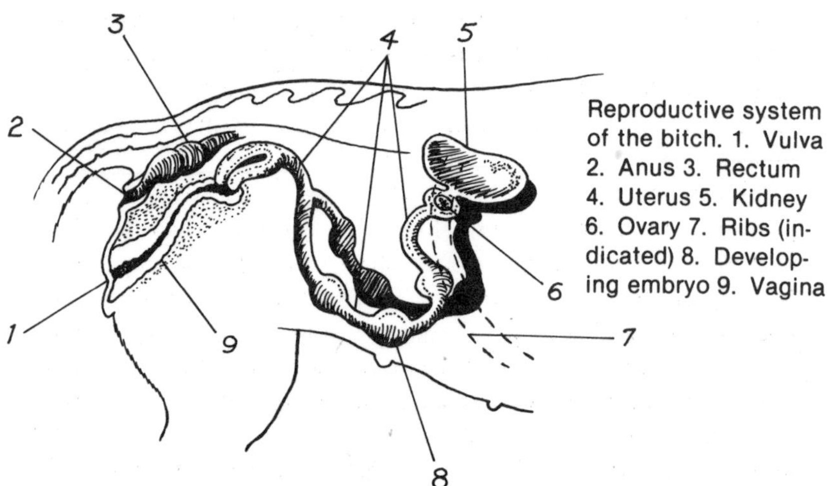

Reproductive system of the bitch. 1. Vulva 2. Anus 3. Rectum 4. Uterus 5. Kidney 6. Ovary 7. Ribs (indicated) 8. Developing embryo 9. Vagina

The Basenji's heat season differs from that of the bitch of any other breed. She comes into heat only once a year, in the autumn, while females of other breeds come into heat usually twice a year, in the spring and fall.

The angle of the vagina as it extends upward from the vulva varies with the particular individual and may be associated with some difficulty in mating. However, the position of the vulva can be voluntarily adjusted to some degree, thus aiding entry of the dog's penis. The vulva contains erectile tissue, swelling markedly when the bitch is in heat. This enlargement of the vulva also facilitates breeding.

Mammary gland activity is associated with the bitch's heat season (i.e. her estrus cycle). Usually ten teats can be counted, five on each side. A bitch could have an additional number of teats. Each teat has six to twelve excretory openings. When the bitch is lactating, the rear teats are larger and usually produce more milk.

IN SEASON, IN HEAT, IN ESTRUS

The bitch's first heat season occurs when she is about eight months old (with a range of six to nine months), then recurs, usually in the spring and fall, every six to eight months thereafter. Curiously enough, however, autumn—just once a year—is the only heat season for the Basenji bitch. Eight-month-old bitches are immature and should not be mated the first heat season. In general, small breeds mature earlier than the large breeds and experience their first heat at an earlier age.

When a bitch nears her heat season, or is in estrus, her vulva swells somewhat and ovulation classically occurs on the twelfth day of heat. During the early portion of the heat season, the bitch becomes very playful with other dogs, but does not generally allow mating yet. Such pre-mating activity can run from three to twenty-seven days, although it is usually between seven to ten days. Many bitches, in their first heat, may show hardly any evidence of discharge. The bloody vaginal discharge which marks the beginning of estrus is caused by congestion and bleeding of the endometrium

Onset of the bitch's heat season is marked by slight swelling of the vulva and a bloody vaginal discharge. Usually around the tenth day of estrus she is ready to mate.

In heat the bitch's vulva becomes markedly swollen. During the days most favorable to mating, it is softer and flabbier, facilitating penetration by the stud.

(the mucous membrane lining the uterus). This heat season, or estrus, lasts about twenty-one days. It is only between the tenth day and the end of the season that most bitches accept males. The male experiences no such cycling of his sexual activity, however, and will be drawn to the female during all phases of her heat cycle.

Most successful matings can be expected to occur from the tenth to the fourteenth day of the heat cycle; it is during this period that ovulation classically occurs. Pregnancy can occur several days after ovulation, however, because the expected longevity of the ova is forty-eight hours and there is a twenty-four hour longevity of the spermatozoa in the female reproductive tract. During the period when the bitch accepts a male, the vulva is softer and flabbier. During the next two months the vulva becomes progressively more normal in size, unless the bitch is in whelp. After a three-to-six month resting phase, the estrus cycle starts again. Assuming that the mating has taken place, let's look at the situation in the bitch that has conceived.

During the first ten to fifteen days of heat, mature ova grow towards the surface of the ovary, from which they protrude as fluid-filled follicles. Once these follicles burst, mature ova are released into the surrounding capsule (fallopian tube) where they then proceed into the uterine horn.

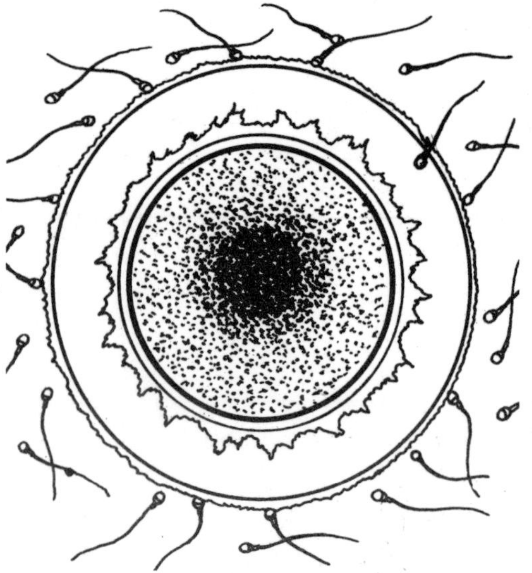

Thousands of sperm cells attempt to penetrate the outer layer of the ovum to fertilize it. Only one is necessary for fertilization. With penetration of the first sperm cell, the full complement of chromosomes (stated simply, the ovum contains half, the sperm carries the other half) necessary for creation of a new fetus is complete. No other spermatozoa are now able to penetrate the egg.

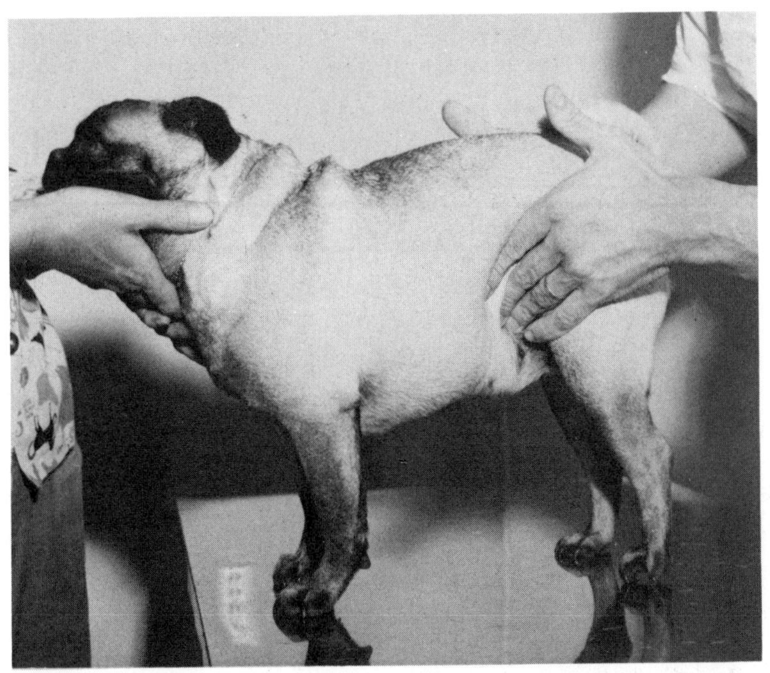

Feeling the golf ball-size fetuses during the third to fourth week of gestation in the uterine horns of the bitch is one of the best ways to determine pregnancy. Beyond this time, they cannot be as easily palpated. However, the fetuses can be easily damaged by the probing, so it should be done by a veterinarian.

While ova are being disseminated throughout the uterine horns, thousands, even millions, of actively swimming sperm cells are brushing against the ova in an attempt to penetrate the egg cell. Only one sperm cell will successfully penetrate the outer surface of the ovum to fertilize it. It is not known why additional spermatozoa can no longer penetrate the ovum once fertilization has occurred, but once the ovum contains a full complement of chromosomes (one-half from the ovum and one-half from the sperm cell), further penetration by other spermatozoa does not occur. Ova that have become successfully fertilized attach to the wall of the uterus where they grow for the next two months. About three weeks after fertilization the fetuses can be felt within the uterine horns as being about the size of a large marble. Feeling these large "marbles" or "golf balls" is one of the best ways to diagnose pregnancy during the third and fourth week of gestation. (To avoid possible damage to the fetuses, this probing should *only* be attempted by a veterinarian.) After this time the fetuses are no longer felt as solid discrete objects and are not as easily palpated. After a total of about 63 days of gestation, the pups are born, or as we say, the bitch whelps. These pups, or whelps, are usually weaned at six weeks of age. The bitch will generally stop lactating within a week after the pups are weaned.

Examining a vaginal smear from the bitch microscopically is the surest way to tell at what point during her estrus cycle she can be bred most successfully.

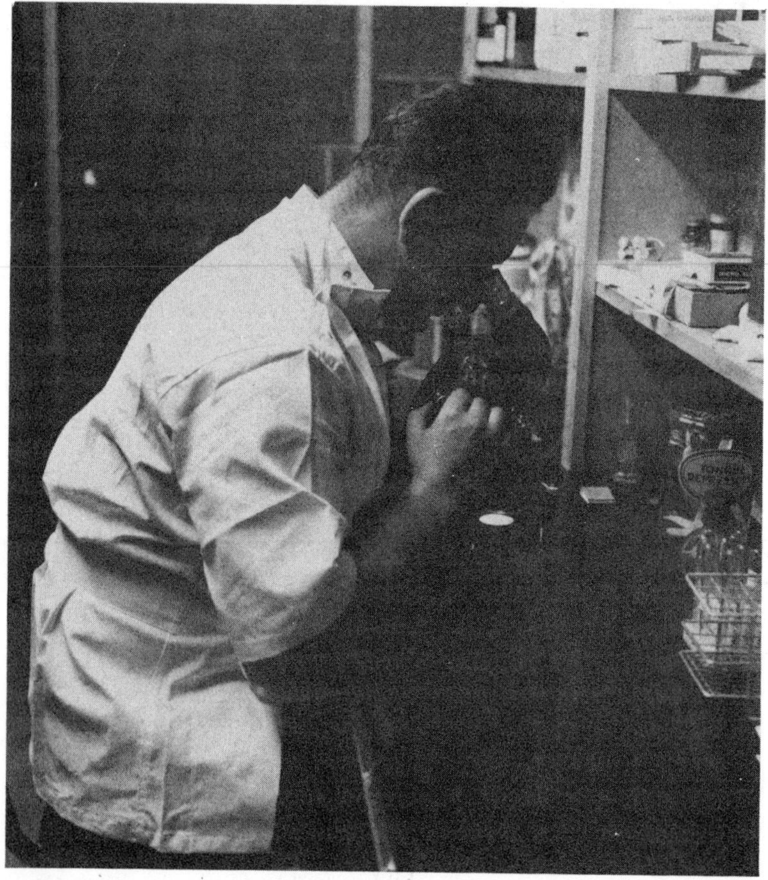

A FEW PROBLEMS

The deficiency of the hormone that stimulates ovulation may cause an abnormally long heat season. Medication can correct this, but the condition will often repeat itself in following periods of heat. A few bitches may come into season on their first heat without giving off any marked external signs; nonetheless, they will readily accept males. You must watch these females especially closely to avoid an unwanted pregnancy.

A hormone deficiency is invariably the cause of bitches failing to come into season at the normal time; they will sometimes wait until they are eighteen to twenty-four months old before they have their first season. Your veterinarian can probably correct this hormonal deficiency, but often this is not the answer to a successful breeding. As a general comment here, note that the use of hormones to prevent coming into heat has not yet been proven to be a good practice. Sterility is often a very complicated biological problem and hormonal balance—and the bitch's whole reproductive life—is easily upset once you start unnatural procedures.

PHYSIOLOGICAL GUESSWORK

The best time for mating is as near to the time of ovulation as possible, which coincides with the midpoint of the time when the bitch is receptive. Outguessing the lifespan of ova and sperm cells is difficult. Most researchers feel the ova remain viable up to about forty-eight hours; however, in some instances they may survive for up to three to five days. Furthermore, not all ova are discharged at the same time. Sperm cells live about three or four days inside the female reproductive tract, but are not always capable of fertilizing ova after the first two days. It may appear difficult *not* to have a successful breeding, but in most cases failure appears to be due to delayed acceptance of the stud by the bitch.

A better indication for dog honeymoon plans would be to rely upon a veterinarian's interpretation of a vaginal smear. By microscopic examination of the stained cells that line the vagina, a diagnostician can determine the best time during the estrus cycle for a successful breeding. This quick diagnostic test is especially valuable in instances where the stud and bitch are not readily available to one another.

A bitch in estrus and ready to mate will generally cock her tail and stand ready for the stud at the slightest touch on the lower back.

Behavior, too, indicates readiness. Males, particularly the young (six to ten months old) inexperienced studs will set up a howl when they detect a bitch who is ready. Curiously enough, dogs with testicular problems (cryptorchids and monorchids) will also be the heralds of the mating season.

The bitch becomes restless, urinates often and may crave more food (but don't overfeed). She cavorts about with other bitches in the kennel, twisting and holding her tail to one side of her vulva when touched anywhere near her genetalia. She also is apt to mount other females, as well as allowing them to mount her. Usually, however, she will not accept males until she is ready. Periodic attempts at breeding can be started early in the bitch's heat but generally she won't allow mating in the early stages—her vagina is too sensitive. It is when her vulva becomes soft and flabby that she accepts the male. Test the bitch by setting your hand gently on her back, above the root of her tail, or touch her vulva. If she stands rigidly and twists her tail from side to side it is a good sign that she will probably be ready to mate.

The glucose fertility test can help you determine the right time for mating the larger dog breeds, but it is more difficult to conduct this test with the smaller breeds and is often inaccurate. Upon ovulation, glucose is normally present in the vaginal secretions. It can be detected using the same indicator tapes used to check for glucose in the urine of diabetic patients. To conduct this simple test, insert a piece of glucose-detection tape into the vagina; if it turns green within a minute, then she is ready to mate twenty-four hours later. If there is not enough vaginal secretion, just the edges of the tape may change color. Remember, however, that this test is not always accurate and you may get a false positive reaction.

PREPARATION OF THE BITCH PRIOR TO BREEDING

Good health does not occur overnight and a prerequisite for successful breeding is good health. Health is relative and so is achievement—the higher the state of health, the greater the success is likely to be. Care of the brood bitch begins months prior to her coming into heat. Making sure the bitch receives a quality diet and is free from chronic (often hidden) diseases is extremely important. The stress of pregnancy is a serious enough drain on the strength of the bitch without compromising her with other stresses. A good state of health will assure greater success of her ability to come into heat, support the fetuses and give birth to healthy offspring.

Two months prior to her expected heat cycle, a complete physical examination including blood tests for heartworms and brucellosis is advisable. A urinalysis should also be conducted to determine if there are any latent urogenital disorders. A stool specimen should also be taken to the veterinarian so you can obtain an accurate identification of the intestinal parasites and receive the proper instructions and medications for effective therapy. All external parasites should also be eliminated at this time.

The bitch contemplated for breeding should undergo a complete physical exam before her heat cycle. Diagnosis of disease or other problems made early can insure enough time for treatment so that the planned mating will not be impeded and the hoped-for pups not endangered.

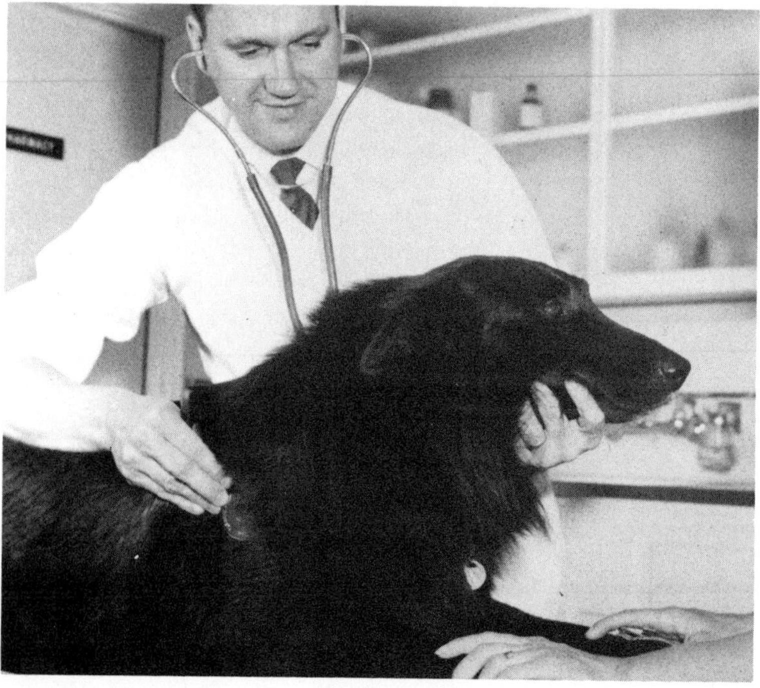

This English Setter bitch projects the good health in which she has been maintained. A continuing state of good health in a bitch you contemplate mating is a necessity, not only to offset the normal strain of pregnancy, but to assure she will come into heat successfully and give birth to healthy pups.

If the disease is properly diagnosed and treatment initiated early enough, most problems can be corrected so that they won't jeopardize the success of the breeding venture. By taking care of these problems prior to the onset of heat you can assure maximum performance by the bitch and minimize the exposure of the puppies to the disease processes.

Periodic examinations of the stud should also be performed, basically for the same reasons outlined for the bitch. If the stud is in poor health you cannot expect him to have the sexual drive and stamina required for good breeding performance.

Virility and excellent physical condition are imperative if a stud dog is to perform well. But he must also embody all the characteristics his breed is prized for and have proven he is a prolific sire as well.

CHAPTER THREE

Courtship and Mating

ABOUT STUD DOGS

A stud means a male dog who mates with a bitch, and specifically, to breeders, means a trained, experienced, and regularly mated dog.

Your stud must not only be typical of his breed, but must excel in whatever he is supposed to be and whatever he is supposed to pass on to his pups. Top physical condition is also important as a pre-mating qualification. He must be selected for his masculinity and virility, temperament, and vigor; he must be prolific and come from a long-lived line so that he has time to be recognized as a good stud after many successful litters. A fine stud is best known by the overall excellence of his pups. Although good studs usually throw several fine puppies, good stock calls for consistent, better than average production. But with selection, as with any expert, there are experts and there are experts. In the breakdown, we have four kinds of studs: experienced and go-getter, average, faint-hearted, and dullard.

THE EXPERIENCED STUD

The easiest dog to handle is the experienced stud. He knows his job and does it with verve, but may even have to be restrained when working with a nervous or a maiden bitch.

THE AVERAGE DOG

The average dog knows his business, too, but usually needs to do some courting first. When ready, he mounts his bitch and does a professional job. He is aware that his handler will help with problem bitches because he has been taught from his first matings to expect help. Every bitch brought to him, regardless of size, will be served.

THE FAINT-HEARTED

Another type of dog is the untrained, perhaps spoiled, but otherwise serviceable male who needs some encouragement. Never mate him to a difficult bitch, at least at first. Such a dog is easily turned away by the bitch. Several bitches in close succession, however, can train this kind of dog to become a passable stud.

THE DULLARD

Then there is the dullard who can usually guess how to mate, and may even be lucky enough to guess which end to mount!

Some breeders expend great patience on such dogs if they represent particularly fine specimens, and will even stimulate the dog's penis, if needed, then go to great lengths in helping the dog to use it. Easy bitches are chosen for this kind of training. A few such dull dogs have indeed been encouraged and turned into decent studs.

A perfectly usable stud may be timid the first time and put off easily by an aggressive bitch. Breeding to several bitches in a short time span should induce better performance.

Every stud, whether a dullard or not, should be trained for his work. The first mating experience should be when he is about ten months old. Choose a good-natured, *experienced* bitch who is ready for mating—just standing there and twisting her tail from side to side. One of the stud's kennel mates is a good choice.

Make sure that the stud has not just been exposed to bitches in season; this reduces his interest. Also, dogs who have just eaten mate more readily, so feed him. If a male is shy, bring the bitch to his quarters.

Allow adequate courting time. Do not rush. Be quiet. Lower the light intensity if the room is too bright.

If there is no activity, encourage your stud. Or, pretend to remove the bitch, perhaps taking her away for a few moments, then return with her with much ado about it all. Work his interest up to fever pitch. He will doubtlessly take the last step all by himself.

The trick now is to accustom your trainee to your meddling in his sex life. The result is that, once he grows up to be a reputable stud, he will turn to you or his handler for help with nasty or otherwise problematical bitches.

Be somewhat intrusive when he tries to mount the bitch. Place your hand on his hindquarters just below his tail. He will probably be annoyed enough to stop, get off and make another pass at mounting. Keep touching and "helping" him in a passive way just so he gets used to your interference—which soon becomes your *assistance* as he comes to consider your part of his amorous undertakings. Some breeders so train their studs that the dogs actually seem to expect help.

THE MATING COSTS AND ARRANGEMENTS

Unproven stud dogs may be permitted to serve a proven bitch free of charge so that his owner can prove that his stud has produced live puppies. The owner then sets a stud fee according to the fees being asked for similar dogs of that breed. Stud fees vary according to breed, the popular and rarer breeds being highest. The champion status of the stud may also be reflected in the stud fee. Bear in mind, however, that the classiest, costliest dogs do not always produce the best pups. The stud fee is paid at the time of the service, independent of the number of pups conceived, or even

The shipping crate in which a bitch will travel should have nothing in it which can catch in the collar and possibly cause her to strangle. Accompany her to the airport or bus terminal, shipping by the most direct route possible, devoid of layovers.

if there is no litter at all. The owner of the stud dog writes a receipt and issues a pedigree of his stud.

Studs usually give a free, repeat performance the next time the bitch is in heat, if she failed to produce a litter from the first attempt. Send or bring the bitch as before to the stud dog. The owner of the bitch should offer to pay the stud owner for this additional expense of lodging the bitch again. There are kennels, however, which charge a regular boarding fee for the bitch during the first mating trip; it is at their discretion whether they charge again for the second, free, mating.

As a rule, a responsible owner of a stud dog not only guarantees that his dog is a proven sire, free from infection, not overused or mated to another bitch just before your bitch, but also guarantees that your bitch will be properly cared for while boarding at his kennel.

The owner of the stud and the owner of the bitch often arrange that the stud owner may choose one pup from the litter, usually when it is six to nine weeks old. In this case, there may not be any stud fee. Be certain to consider two possibilities: the bitch has no puppies or she has only one puppy. The solution? Write down the agreement! Avoid misunderstandings later. Should the puppyless bitch owner retroactively pay a stud fee? If only one pup is born, will the dogs be mated again at no charge? And so on.

THE TRAVELING BITCH

The bitch should receive only a very small amount of food and water prior to shipping. Motion sickness and nausea are much more likely to occur if a large meal is consumed just prior to shipping. You may want to send a supply of food outside her box in the event that there is a transportation mix-up, but food should not be left inside the shipping box. As an extra precaution, add an extra address tag under the bedding just in case the other labels are lost. Still another label declaring "valuable dog" should be conspicuously and permanently stuck onto the shipping box. For nervous dogs, check with your veterinarian about sedatives, but be careful that oversedation does not occur. It can ruin or even kill your dog.

Accompanying your bitch should be a note about her idiosyncracies, traveling times, her pet name, as well as some completely filled out return address labels. She should be wearing her collar, with identification, and her lead should be in the box, but not in such a way as to strangle her. Also, be sure there is nothing in the shipping crate that might catch on her collar. For long trips, send her by air; she will arrive in better shape. If possible, accompany the bitch to the airport, train or bus terminal, or at least try to witness her being shipped. Ship her by the most direct, fastest route and avoid en route layovers or transfers.

When a bitch arrives for breeding, the stud owner cares for his stud's guest for several days. Upon arrival she is fed, watered and given some exercise. She must, at all times, be well guarded. On the following day after any nervousness has been overcome, she is

The carrying case you choose for your dog will depend on its size and your preference. The Peke, because of its small size, is well served by a light weight rattan.

mated (if she will accept the male) and returned to her box or to a kennel. Breeders should mate the bitch again 48 hours later. It is a nice gesture on the part of the stud owner to telephone the bitch's owner and report that the mating took place and all is well.

The stud owner may keep a visiting bitch until her season is over, thus assuring themselves (and the good names of their studs) that the resulting pups are in fact those of their own studs.

THE BITCH IN HEAT

In season, the bitch's urine greatly excites dogs and attracts hopeful suitors for miles around. Even chain-link fencing has failed to prevent fruitful mating of stud and bitch. Products are available to make bitches less attractive to males, but kennel dogs may soon be conditioned to the odor of the "de-scenter" and realize that it means "in heat." Chlorophyll-containing tablets, given orally, are at least helpful in reducing the range from which potential males are aroused. Doggie sanitary napkins, too, are available for keeping your home clean while your bitch is in season. Keep the bitch, especially an older one, warm, out of drafts and off of cold, wet grass or chilly floors.

MATING EQUIPMENT

Handlers should wear leather gloves to prevent being bitten during the course of difficult matings.

Mounting blocks, especially when each of the mating couple is of a different size, are desirable: use a filled sack, straw bale, a dug-

A number of commercial items are available to counteract the odor of the bitch in heat and discourage unwanted male dogs that threaten undesirable matings. Also sold are paraphernalia to keep in-season females from staining rugs, furniture fabric, etc.

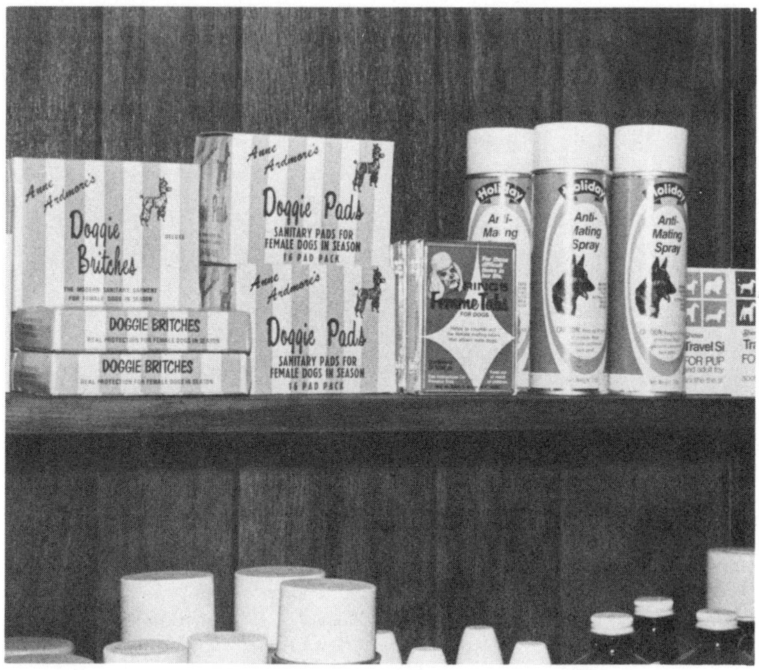

out step in the garden to make an earth platform, or a table. The bitch's collar and lead must be leather, and *never* be a choke collar or chain lead.

A muzzle made from a bandage strip is useful if the bitch snaps and is overly nasty. If there are two handlers, however, do not bother muzzling the bitch. One handler loops the end of a leash over the muzzle of the bitch and holds it taut under her chin, thus letting her move ahead but still remain under the control of the handler. This is less frustrating for the bitch who is unaccustomed to being muzzled.

Maiden bitches should be examined for vaginal stricture. If necessary, petroleum jelly can be used as a lubricant. Large kennel breeders, when dealing with such a stricture, may resort to hollow, uterine bougies for use with nervous bitches who refuse to stand for the dog. When the vulva is completely flabby (indicating more accurately than anything else that the bitch is ready), it is very gradually dilated with a bougie (warmed to body temperature) until the opening is large enough to fit the dog's penis. We repeat: do not use a bougie unless the vulva is *completely* soft at the top and very flabby. A lubricated finger or two can also be used to dilate a stricture. Stubborn strictures should be corrected by a veterinarian.

During the "getting to know" period, the maiden bitch may decide she's not going to cooperate . . .

. . . and will not accept the stud without first being muzzled.

After the bitch has been subdued, the "getting to know" process continues more peacefully.

When the stud and bitch meet for the first time, give the pair time to get to know each other.

THE MATING PLACE

The stud usually mates better at home, the bitch being brought to him. By conditioning the stud to mating in the same place each time, he realizes what is expected of him there. Keep the mating place as empty as possible so the stud can delineate his territory by applying his scent around it. When a male seems to want privacy before performing, the owner should still keep an eye on things, even if through a window or a peephole in the wall; he must be a witness to the act, not to speak of helping out if needed by a poor stud who is set upon by his unwilling mistress.

STUD MEETS BITCH

Let the stud and bitch—both wearing leather collars—get to know each other. The stud is on his own home ground and knows why the bitch is there. The bitch, on the other hand, is not at home and is perhaps apprehensive at first. When it is obvious that the two dogs are quite interested in doing what they are there for, encourage them to urinate and then lead them to where they are expected to mate. If the bitch must be muzzled (not often necessary), do it just before the second meeting. The handler of the bitch—when she is big—should wear gloves and hold the lead securely in case she is scared and attacks the stud, or perhaps even the handler. Keep the leads taut so each handler can pull his dog away in the event of trouble. If the bitch is ready, however, there is usually no trouble. Timid bitches may at first hide behind something, growling and showing their teeth. Continual refusal of a bitch may mean she is not quite ready. Or, the right time may even be past. Some very spoiled bitches may appear to be frigid. This is sometimes the result of the bitch's overdevotion to her owner. Try mating this apparently frigid bitch out of sight of her owner and the chances are she will thaw out and the mating will be a success.

THE TIE (USING THREE HANDLERS)

The stud tries several times to mount, searching with his penis for the vulva. He keeps up with a rhythmic pumping motion until he penetrates, then vigorously thrusts and retracts several times until he is "tied" to the bitch. This is when the bulbous enlarge-

Breeding large dogs may require three handlers. Two of the handlers seat themselves on either side of the bitch, grasping each other's wrists underneath her abdomen to keep her from squatting after penetration. The third handler is present to give help as it is needed.

ment of the penis expands within the vaginal cavity and cannot be withdrawn. If a bitch becomes excited and moves around, her handler verbally quiets her. The third handler prevents her from squatting (by supporting her with his knee under her) if she tries to do that just after the stud penetrates. The second handler keeps them from pulling apart. The stud practically dances on his hind legs as his semen (containing the sperm) is ejaculated. He then rests on the bitch's back, his forepaws clasped around her, panting from exertion and resting his head on the bitch's neck, perhaps licking her ears and eyes affectionately. Some studs gnash and grind their teeth. Young studs may regurgitate out of excitement. A few excitable studs work themselves up so much that they ac-

Supporting the bitch with a knee underneath her after the tie has taken place prevents her from crouching and possibly damaging the stud's genitalia.

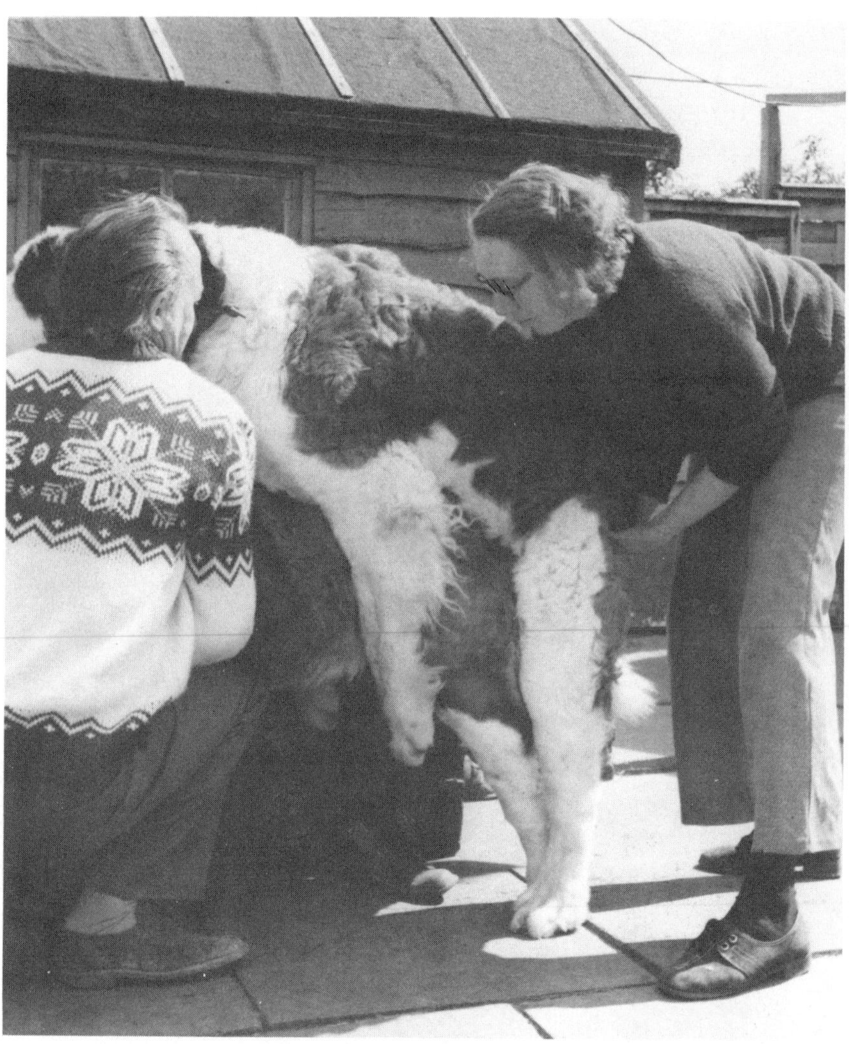

The presence of three handlers for the largest breeds is particularly important as the dogs' weight could cause them to seriously injure themselves if one were to fall or the bitch to crouch. Here, two of these St. Bernard breeders employ the grasped wrists method mentioned previously, while the third gives an assist to make sure the stud does not fall.

tually tumble over backwards. Soothing talk quiets the dogs and helps prevent the male from dismounting until the "tie" occurs.

Once tied, the stud, now restless, dismounts for the duration of the tie. Although the couple may stand side by side while the tie lasts, the stud usually "turns." To turn the stud, if he cannot do it alone, the handler lifts the dog's closest hind leg and passes it gently over the back of the bitch until the leg is right around on the ground on the other side, thus leaving the two dogs standing back to back. The important thing is that, whether side by side or turned, they must not pull themselves apart; this might cause serious injury, particularly to the stud's reproductive apparatus. Tied dogs may stay that way from several seconds to over an hour. Pregnancy *can* result without a tie.

While waiting for the tie to break, the two handlers make themselves comfortable and hold their respective dogs. Both dogs are now calm. The third handler can act as relief. The handlers do not

After he has penetrated, the stud thrusts vigorously several times until the tie takes place.

The stud will turn, after the tie, to stand beside the bitch, or back to back. At this point, he may need some help in swinging one leg over the bitch's hindquarters to make the turn.

allow the bitch to sit as she may damage the male's organ.

The foregoing description of mating was with three handlers. Mating of large breeds should be under complete control, and three handlers are often used—one to control the bitch, one to control the stud, and one to direct the whole operation.

TWO HANDLERS

A difficult bitch can be managed with two handlers if a third is unavailable. Tether the bitch on a very short lead. The two handlers sit on their stools on either side of the bitch and grasp each others' wrists under her to prevent her from squatting. The stud handler uses his free hand to manage his dog. Likewise, the handler of the bitch uses his free hand for controlling his dog, or, if need be, to guide his bitch's vulva to the stud. In larger breeds, the handlers support the bitch on their flexed knees under her abdomen, keeping both hands free to aid the dogs if necessary.

MANAGING WITH ONE HANDLER

Young maiden bitches or inexperienced studs can make a difficult situation for one handler. Large bitches can be tethered to a ring or door handle with the lead as short as possible and with the body against the wall. The handler, sitting on a stool, can usually prevent the bitch from squatting by placing one or both knees under her, thus leaving his hands free, one to guide the vulva if need be and the other to hold the stud. Because most studs know their business, when there is one handler he usually spends his time managing the bitch.

Some breeders with small, particularly toy, dogs use an armchair to control their dogs between the back and the two arms of the chair. Toy breeds have also been mated on their owner's lap.

SIZE DIFFERENCES

Although various sized street dogs somehow manage despite any help, there can be problems (beyond the obvious one of the

The mating pair rest quietly after the stud has turned, until the tie is broken and he is able to withdraw from the bitch.

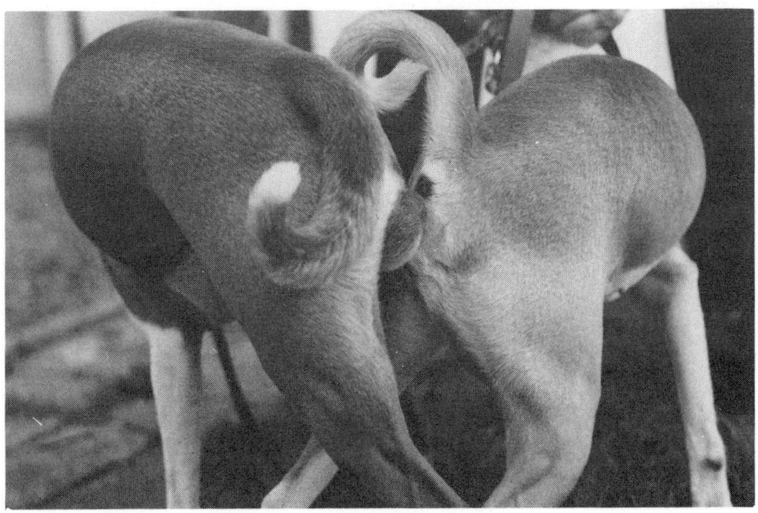

smaller male reaching a larger female) such as penis size and the slope of the vagina. Studs are normally larger than bitches of the same breed; such mating is no problem. Toy breeds, however, may involve mating a tiny stud to a much larger bitch. The owner can help by providing the stud with a non-skid platform or by holding him up after the turn if his legs do not reach the ground. The much bigger bitch's constrictor muscles may not be tight enough to hold the stud, and some toy breed owners hold the dog on the back of the bitch with the bitch well supported to tolerate this extra weight.

AFTER THE TIE

When the stud is freed of the bitch, ascertain that his penis has returned to its sheath. If it has not, the exposed membrane may dry out before the organ returns to normal size. A cloth, wrung

This breeder holds her Chihuahua bitch on its back after mating to facilitate the flow of semen up the uterine horns.

Breeders of toy dogs can use an armchair (or even their lap) to mate their dogs. This Chihuahua breeder uses her leg to help control the activity of her dogs.

out in cold water and gently applied, keeps the membrane moist and helps reduce the swelling so the organ can return to its sheath. Some breeders have a quicker method with no apparent discomfort to the dog: a glass of cold water is kept ready during mating. A dog's exposed penis, which has not returned immediately to his sheath, is dipped for a second or two into the cold water. The organ contracts and quickly returns to its sheath, thus saving the delicate penis from exposure.

Keep the stud away from other dogs awhile because other studs will sense he mated. This could lead to serious fighting.

Clean up the bitch with absorbent cotton and return her to her box or quarters for several hours (or preferably the next day) before shipping her anywhere. Although she may drink, do not let her relieve herself for an hour or two after mating, if preventable.

When large dogs finish mating, be aware that a large quantity of fluid may drip from the bitch as the male organ is withdrawn.

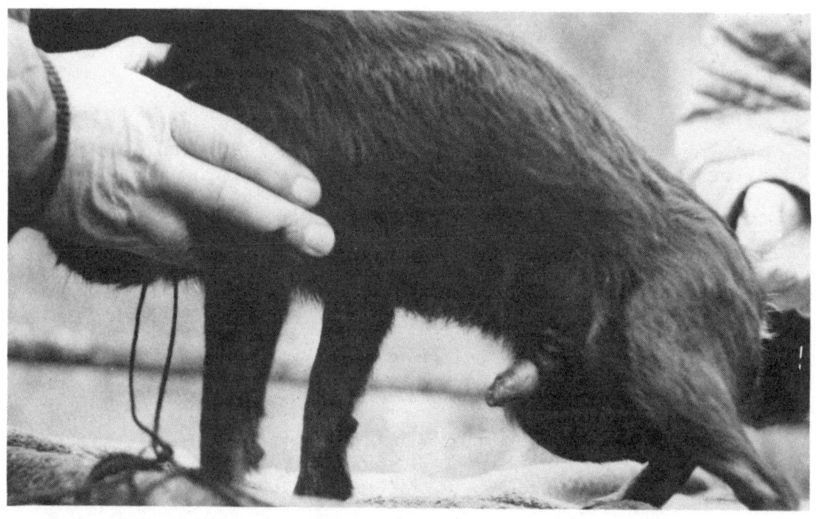

A male dog immediately after he has withdrawn from the female. The penis has not yet retracted into the prepuce. Gently applying a cool damp cloth may hasten the process and prevent the membrane from drying out and injuring the dog.

HORMONAL HELP

Some studs, such as among the bloodhounds, may not show the least spark of mating drive. A veterinarian may be able to help by administering the appropriate hormonal medication.

ARTIFICIAL INSEMINATION

Artificial insemination is frowned upon and even prohibited in some cases, but it may be useful at times. Semen taken from a stud after he reaches maturity is injected or infiltrated by means of an inseminating rod and syringe into the reproductive tract of a bitch who is at the right stage of estrus. The semen can be carefully placed into the vagina or even into the cervix and uterus of the bitch. Some authorities consider it safer to infiltrate the semen by gravity, rather than injecting it, to obviate injury to the sperm cells by the force of injection. Semen has been preserved successfully for about a week and stored for a year (and still maintained 50 per cent motility). Before artificial insemination is used, the rules and restrictions of the American Kennel Club should be consulted.

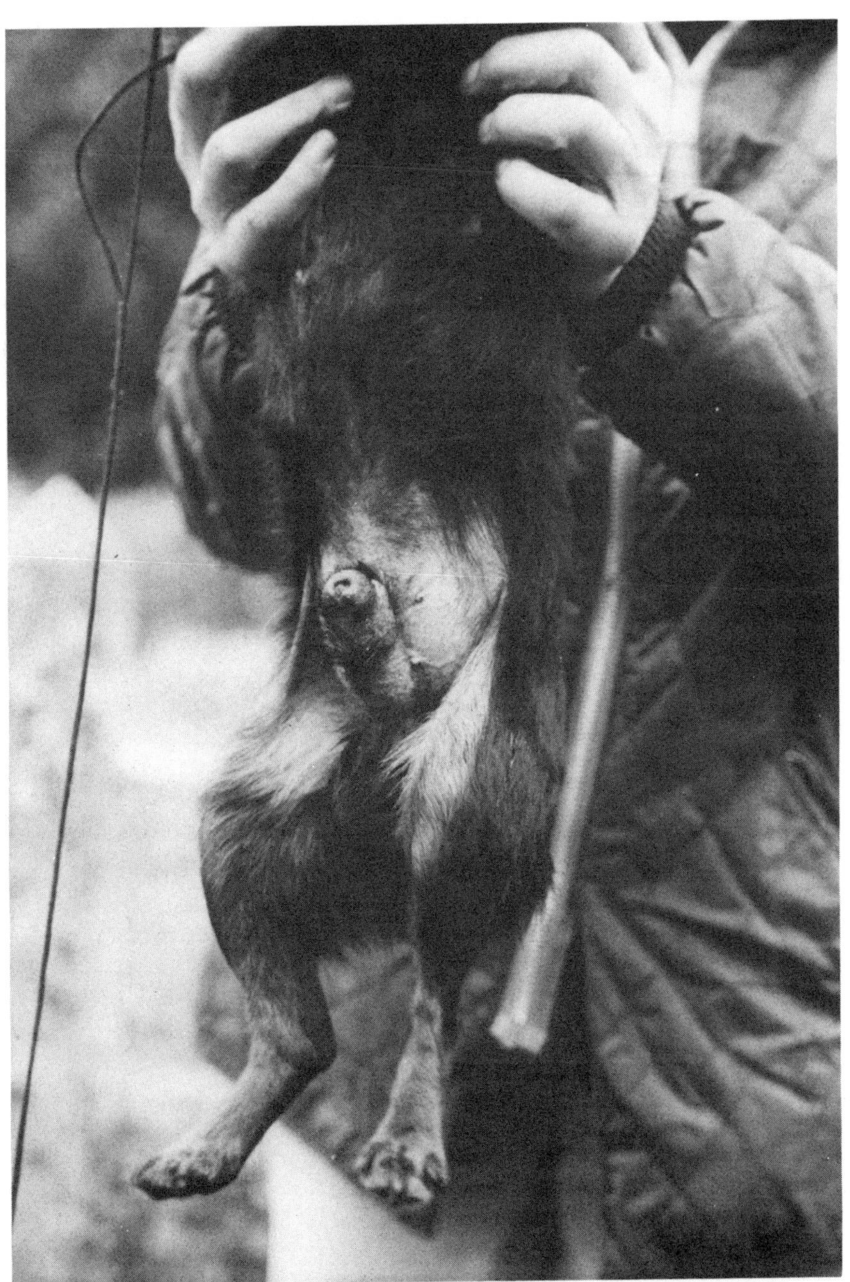

The stud returned to normal after mating. The penis is fully sheathed again.

Not every mating will be love at first sight as seems to be the case with these English Setters. While the experienced stud or bitch will know what the business at hand is and carry through on it, the spoiled bitch or inexperienced stud may need coaxing, or just plain refuse to complete the mating.

CHAPTER FOUR

What's Going Wrong?

The over-enthusiastic stud may rush so much that he ejaculates without penetrating the bitch, or he doesn't penetrate enough. His penis is exposed, the bulb enlarged and the semen still being ejected. Allow him to mount the bitch at once and he will continue pumping, thus causing the penis to return to its normal size and slip back into its sheath again. Or, the cold water technique described under *After the Tie* above can be used. The stud will probably mount the bitch again to mate without any trouble this time.

If the end of his penis is not returned to the sheath, apply some petroleum jelly gently to the area, then carefully draw the sheath forward until the penis is in place again. If the organ is too swollen for this maneuver, call a veterinarian.

If you try to turn the stud before the prepuce is completely pushed back behind the bulb, he will howl with pain; leave him as he is on top of the bitch, but you may have to support them somewhat until the situation subsides.

MESALLIANCE

Breeding with an undesirable male (either a mongrel or another breed) does not affect any future litter of that bitch. Possible pregnancy can be terminated by a timely injection by a veterinarian. The bitch should not be mated again that season, however.

MULTIPLE CONCEPTIONS

If a bitch copulates with a stud as much as seven or more days after an original mating, she could have pups by both sires. In this case, the names of both of the studs must be presented when the litter is registered at a kennel club. Biologically it is possible for a litter of ten puppies to be the result of ten separate breedings by ten separate males with each puppy being sired by a different stud.

EXTRANEOUS FACTORS

Abrupt environmental changes can cause dogs to be temporarily infertile until they have become accustomed to the change. Cramped, dark quarters tend to decrease fertility, whereas fresh air, sunlight and exercise increase it.

Duration of daylight, which affects the bitch's reproductive cycle, can be controlled in kennels by adjusting the light artificially. Some authorities observed that a procedure of increasing the intensity of the light by one hour daily for the first week, two hours daily for the second week, three hours daily for the third week and four hours daily for the fourth week, almost always brought a bitch into season. If you live in a cold area, February is the best month for mating because the pups benefit from warm spring and summer weather when they are born.

THE FRIGID BITCH

Spoiled pet bitches, especially, may not follow through with their sexual instincts and thus become frigid. Such a bitch may look at a male, but not let him mount her. Although some of these frigid bitches may "work out" after enough patient guidance by the owner, some breeders arrange a forced mating, after which the bitch most likely is receptive at the next meeting.

ROMANCE

A stud and bitch can express individual preferences for mating. A bitch who refuses to stand for one stud will do it at once for another. A bitch has been known to fail to have puppies by more than one proven and pedigreed stud, but to immediately have large litters by mongrels of her own choice.

A stud who refuses to mate a visiting bitch may be made to reconsider by introducing another stud to the bitch at the same time and within full view of the recalcitrant stud, thus causing jealousy and perhaps immediate action.

A stud and bitch introduced for mating may indulge in courting rituals at the outset. During this phase, the stud may be playful and even display affection toward the bitch, nuzzling and licking her about the face and neck. Courtship does not always take place; whether or not it does depends upon the individuals involved.

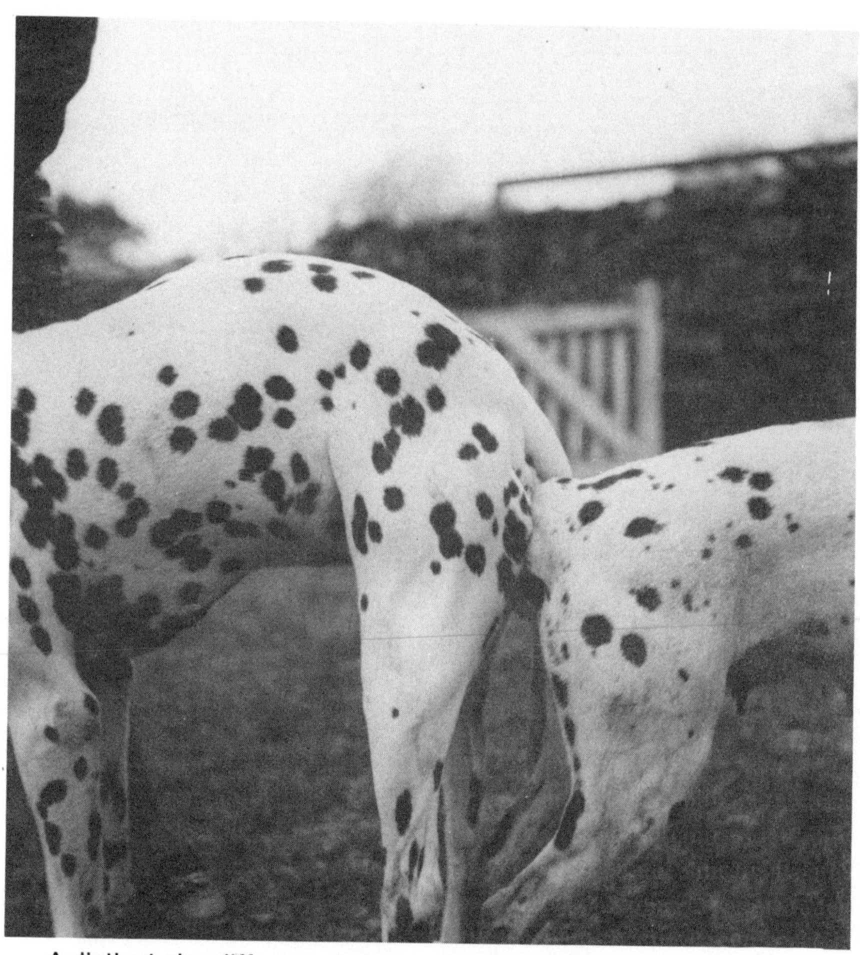

A distinct size difference between the stud and bitch can impede a successful mating. This is particularly true when a very small male is mated to a larger female, because the bitch's constrictor muscles may not be able to hold the smaller dog's penis. The more usual mating of a large stud to a smaller bitch, as is the case with these Dals, causes no problem.

AGE DISPARITY

Although an old stud and an old bitch should not be mated together, an old stud could certainly be mated with a young bitch. A young stud mated to an old bitch, however, would probably not produce a large litter, or could produce no litter at all.

The best results are obtained when both stud and bitch are young adults and in good condition. The bitch's best puppies are generally thrown, or whelped, in her second or third litter, which also are usually her largest litters. A stud of one of the larger breeds usually sires the best pups when he is almost four years old. Small dogs, such as toy breeds, usually reach this point of maximum return when they are somewhat younger.

Too early or too frequent mating tends to decrease fertility in both sexes.

MALNUTRITION—OVER OR UNDER

Lack of protein, inadequate levels of vitamins and minerals, and the absence of other elements of a balanced diet can cause infertility. On the other hand, overfed males become too fat and lazy to make good studs. Obese bitches do not throw litters often. Overly thin dogs may not produce satisfactorily either. Puberty may be delayed in pups who lack an adequate diet during their active growth period. Such pups may grow into adults deprived of normal sexual desire and drive.

Excessive vitamin and mineral supplementation can be as harmful as a deficiency. The answer to good nutrition is balanced nutrition. Through research more is known about canine nutrition than human nutrition. Suitable exercise, too, goes hand in hand with good diet.

HISTORY OF ILLNESS

Severe illness, especially one involving fever, can negatively affect fertility. Canine distemper and canine virus hepatitis can cause infertility. Good studs kept in perfect condition and not overused sometimes suddenly become infertile. Canine brucellosis, a bacterial disease, is a serious cause of sterility in both sexes and is contagious to humans. It's presence can be detected by serological tests. Other reasons for apparent sudden cessation of productivity are not clearly understood yet.

FAINTING

Small, older studs may faint for several seconds during mating. A whiff of smelling salts might save the day. A physical examination and a month or so of rest is prescribed for such a stud.

BEHAVIORAL PROBLEMS IN BREEDING

Oversexed studs may turn infertile unless they get adequate exercise and diversion (hunting, or other kinds of gainful employment). Castration may be the only solution in extreme cases. Even then, behavioral patterns may be so well established that there may be little observable change after the surgery.

FALSE OR PSEUDO-PREGNANCY

Pseudo-pregnancy occurs when a bitch produces no pups from an apparent pregnancy. Sometimes maiden bitches, not matron bitches, may present signs of pregnancy right up to the time calculated for whelping, including nest-building behavior, labor pains and even production of milk. But no puppies arrive. The length of false pregnancy—including the nervousness, lactation, adoption of toys as puppies and the apparent emotional upset can be treated hormonally and thereby shortened, however, this phenomenon may be repeated with subsequent heat cycles. This condition is due to an abnormal hormonal state originating in the ovaries. The bitch can still eventually have a normal litter, but not until the next season.

UNDESCENDED TESTICLES

Some male dogs may be cryptorchids, that is, dogs who have either one or both testicles up in the body rather than descended down into the scrotum. A dog with only one testicle descended is sometimes referred to as a monorchid. Such a dog that has a testicle which has descended only down into the inguinal canal (that is the canal which runs from the abdomen to the scrotum) may be fertile, although still classified by the breeder as cryptorchid. In most pups the testicles descend by six weeks, some by three and

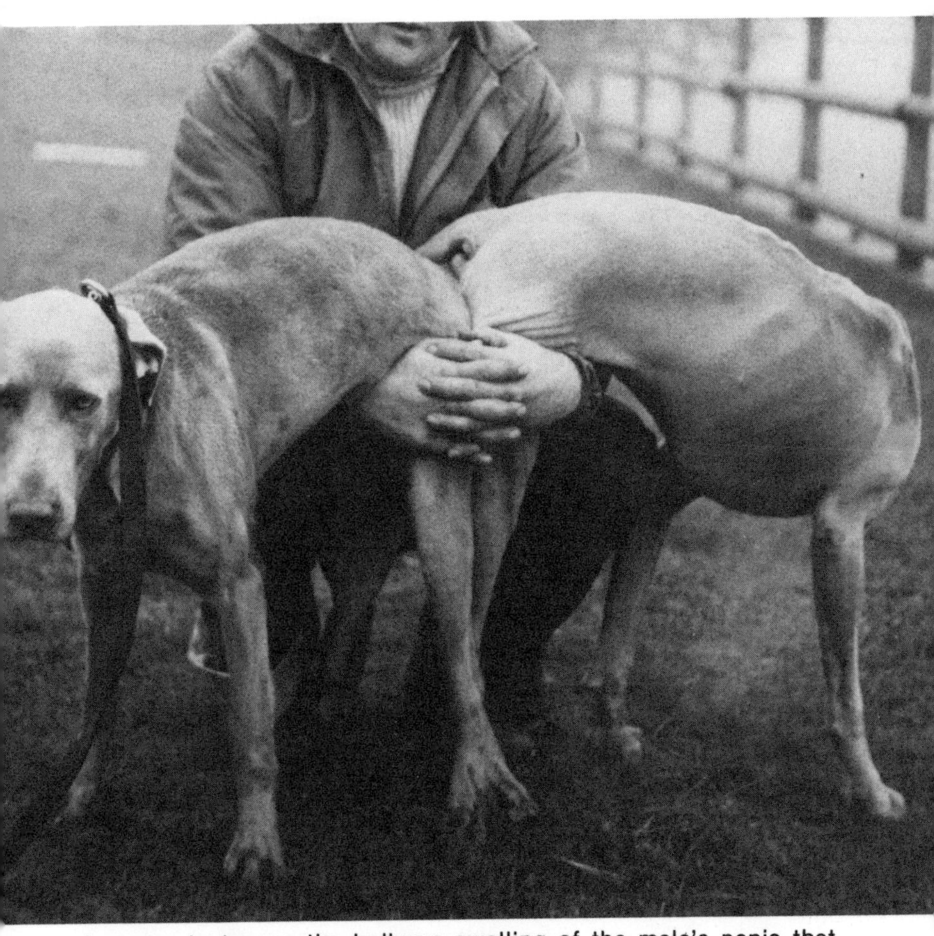

In some instances the bulbous swelling of the male's penis that causes the tie will not take place during a mating. He can still impregnate the bitch but will much more easily slip out of the bitch prematurely. Holding the dogs together will prevent their separating before the sperm has been deposited in the bitch's vagina.

Frequently after mating, dogs and bitches will withdraw to lick themselves clean.

one-half months, and, rarely, may take as long as six months. You can begin to be concerned if you do not detect testicles in your pups by four to six weeks of age. Descent after six months of age is very rare. The condition is inherited, and affected males should never be used for breeding.

OVARIAN GROWTHS

Cysts and tumors growing in the ovary can elicit the symptoms of continual estrus or lack of estrus. Your veterinarian can decide whether medication or surgery is required in such cases.

STERILITY

A bitch may appear not to be ill but continually have difficulties in breeding: poor fertility, puppies which die, unpredictable estrus cycles, abortions, occasional mucopurulent discharge, or other conditions. See your veterinarian for clearing up these problems.

READY VETERINARY HELP

It is necessary to establish a working relationship with a veterinarian of your choice and let him know you are depending on him for his professional help. Above all, take his advice on preventive veterinary medicine. Many of the problems he is called upon to treat could have been prevented had his advice been asked and heeded earlier. Remember, your veterinarian is a highly trained professional—use him when indicated and take his advice.

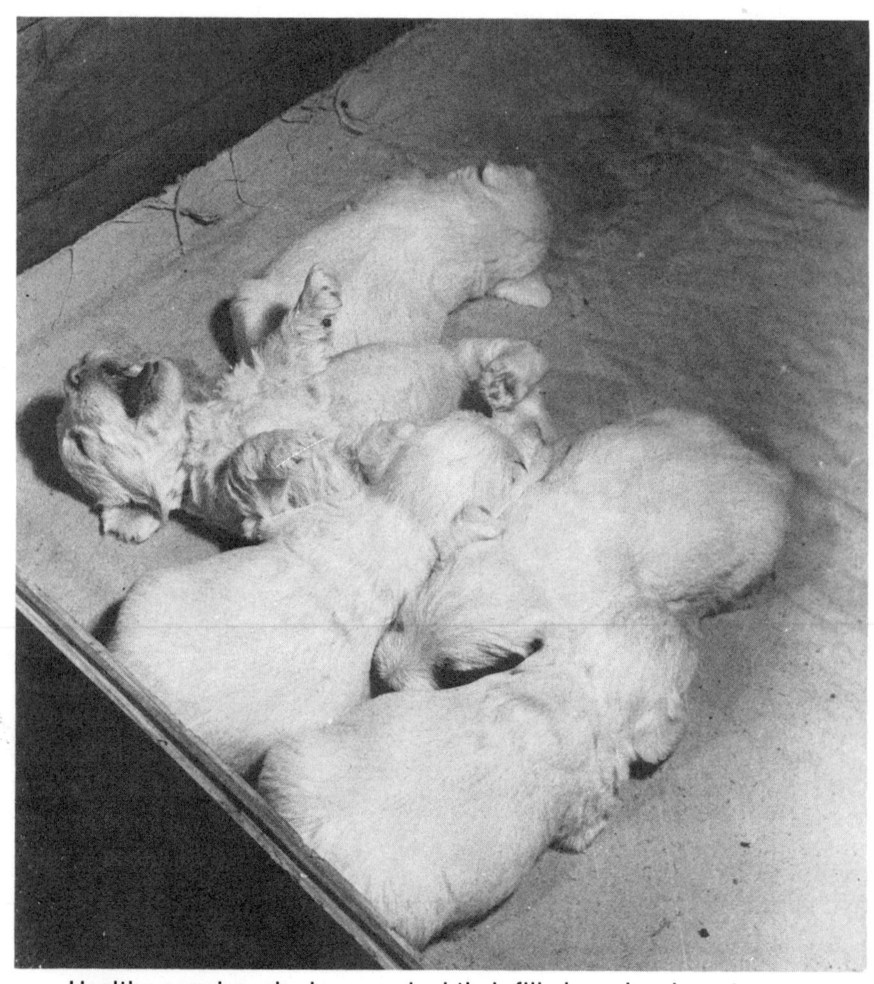

Healthy puppies who have sucked their fill sleep deeply and quietly between feedings.

CHAPTER FIVE

Preparing for Puppies

BEDDING

An old pillowcase filled with clean cotton rags or other clean clothing makes a suitable mattress. A nice, comfortable blanket over this keeps the bitch snug and warm. Even clean newspaper is adequate. Place this bedding in a draft-free and dry area. Beautifully extravagant, as well as economically priced and hygienically adequate dog beds are available commercially. A word of caution: don't use bedding that may become tangled around the bitch or puppies.

GROOMING

Long-coated bitches may lose their coats six weeks or so after whelping. Clipping can be advantageous because puppies have strangled in the tail feathering or other parts of their long coated dam. If you do not clip a long-haired bitch, but fear that the hair is long enough to be dangerous to the pups, give her a hairdo to tie her hair out of harm's way. Hair around teats may need trimming so it does not mat or totally obscure the milk giving orifices that the puppy will seek.

FEEDING

Although some breeders feel the need to add supplemental meat and raw eggs to the diet of the pregnant bitch, this really is not necessary. A quality brand of commercially available dog food is not only adequate, but better balanced than anything you might concoct in your kitchen. Each year hundreds of thousands of dollars are spent for research in the area of canine nutrition. The

The in-whelp bitch's diet requires special attention. A veterinarian can tell you just what vitamin and mineral supplements should be added to her regular food.

knowledge gained through this research is used to compile the complete and balanced diets available in the supermarkets. Of course, not all commercial dog foods are of the same quality. If you are in doubt as to the quality of your brand, ask your veterinarian for guidance.

If the dog is not fat, let her have as much food as she wants (within reasonable limits, of course), although quality is more important than quantity. Quality means balanced nutrition of all the components. If the particular diet you are feeding is not of the best quality, you may want to supplement protein as well as a calcium-phosphorous-vitamin D^2 supplement, but these extra additives must be balanced. Adding just calcium without phosphorous can lead to a mineral imbalance; this is especially a serious problem for growing pups.

Keep your bitch's weight to what can be considered normal for a pregnant dog. Remember, though, she will look big. Fat bitches may have problems whelping.

Too many raw eggs could lead to a deficiency in biotin, a B-group vitamin, synthesized by the dog. A biotin deficiency can

The Doberman Pinscher, powerful and well-muscled, used extensively as a guard dog, is nonetheless required by the breed standard to be neither shy nor vicious. A well-bred Doberman must have a sound temperament, together with its fearlessness and boundless energy.

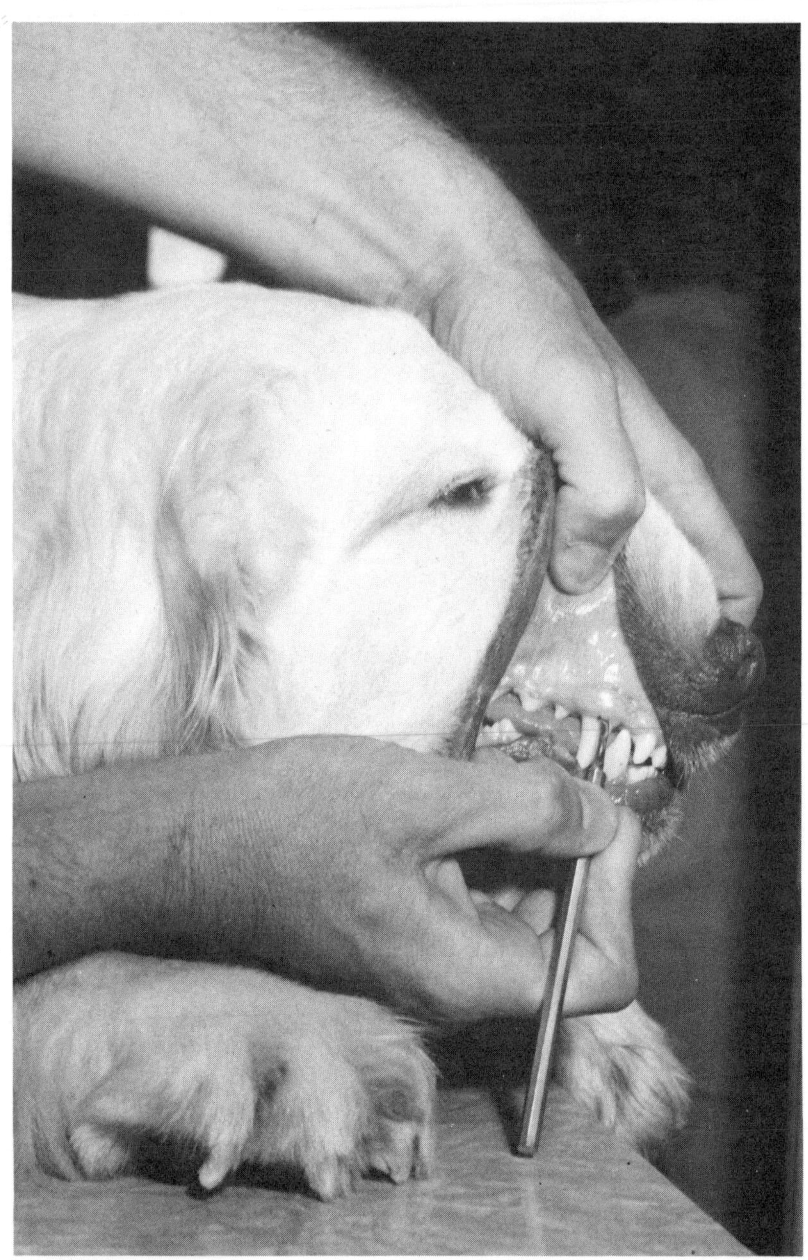

Dog biscuits and dry food help minimize tartar on a dog's teeth, but some dogs have such an excessive build-up of tartar it requires mechanical removal.

be avoided by cooking the egg, or, if you give raw eggs, by giving only the yolk and not the raw white part.

The bitch's diet should be increased by the fourth week of gestation. A bitch needs approximately double the normal amount of food during the latter part of pregnancy and up to three times as much during lactation. Feed (but do not overfeed) the bitch generously from the fifth week on. Divide her meals as she grows larger. Two meals a day is a good beginning, then going to three a day if she is expecting a large litter. Meals that are too moist and which are not accompanied with chewable dry meal or doggie bones allow tartar to accumulate on her teeth. Pet stores have an excellent assortment of doggie bones available to stimulate healthy gums and prevent tartar accumulation. Nylabone® has an added safety feature in that dogs can't chew off and swallow portions which could result in blockage of the intestine. Maintain a fresh supply of water and let her drink as much as she wants.

For breeders or pet owners who feel supplements are necessary to enhance the regular diet of their animals, leading manufacturers have several useful products on the market. Your veterinarian should be consulted before their use.

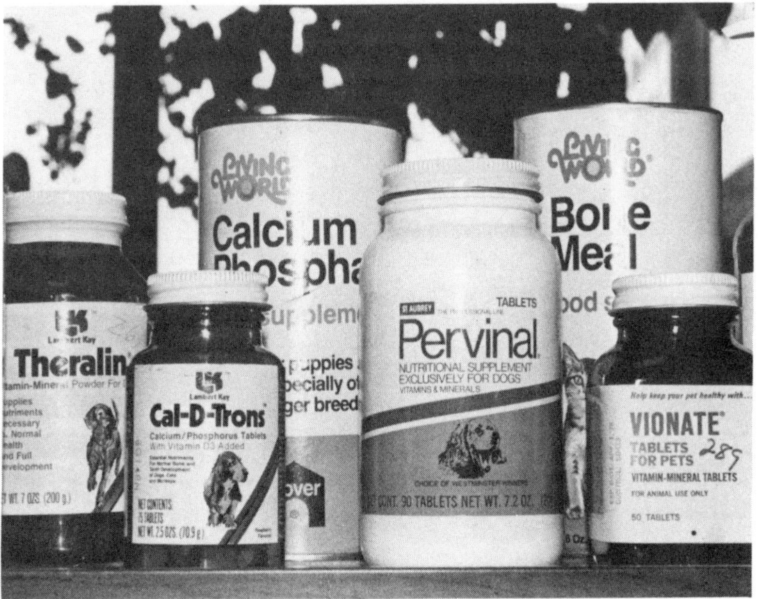

EXERCISE

The pregnant bitch needs her usual exercise until she gets heavy. She is not an invalid. When the end of pregnancy approaches, encourage her going out for a few shorter walks instead of her usual long one. Over-exertion, long car rides, negotiating stairways or jumping up and down on furniture are things that should be avoided.

The in-whelp bitch needs her usual exercise. As she approaches the end of her pregnancy, shorten the length of her walks and don't allow over-exertion.

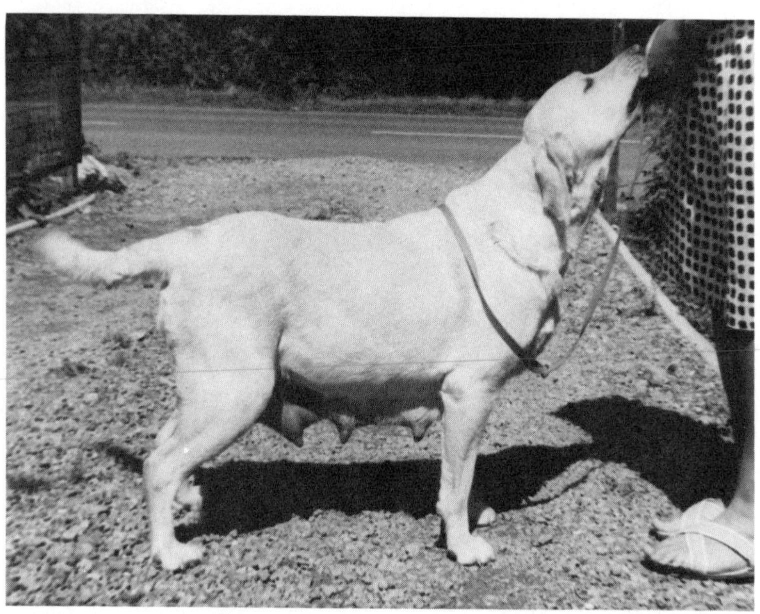

GENERAL CARE OF AN IN-WHELP BITCH

Lift an in-whelp bitch gently, without shoving your fingers into her abdomen. When letting her down on the floor, set her on all fours. However you take hold, depending upon the size of your dog and your size, always lend full support to the puppy-laden abdomen without pressing on it. Sometimes this seems difficult, so don't lift! The bitch herself will let you know if you are hurting her should it become imperative to move her around in this way.

To prevent chills, try not to wash the bitch after the fourth week of mating. If she is so filthy and bedraggled that you must bathe her, dry her completely, keep her in a warm place, and unless you live in a warm climate, be careful about letting her out too soon after washing if she is still damp. Brushing her frequently will keep the coat clean and healthy and usually helps avoid any necessity of bathing.

THE WHELPING BOX

The bitch should have a place of her own in which to give birth to her pups, as well as to stay with them as they begin to go from the newborn to the very young puppy stage. The whelping box is just such a solution. The points to keep in mind when building the box are as follows: the box should be raised several inches off of the ground to keep dampness and drafts from the bitch and her pups; the box should be high enough so that when the bitch lies down in it the draft passes completely over her (that is, it should be no less than a foot high); and the box should be roomy enough for the dog and her puppies to really stretch out in even though they may prefer to cozy up together in one of the corners. This

The whelping box should have a guard rail extending out from the sides of the box to protect the puppies from suffocating if the dam inadvertently rolls back, trapping a pup between herself and the side of box.

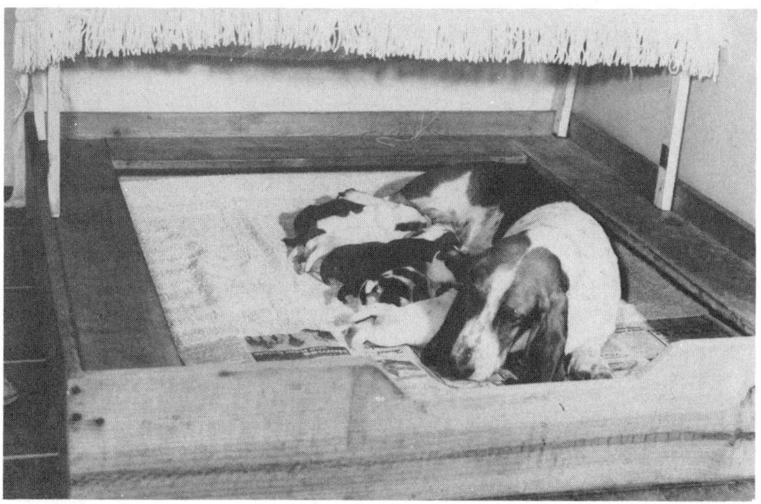

tendency to lay up against the corners brings us to a very important point about the whelping box: it should have a guard rail built around the inside of it. This guard rail is a strip of wood which projects out above the floor of the box so that if the mother should lie up against the side of the box the guard rail keeps her from pressing against the side itself, thus preventing any small puppies from being squashed and suffocated inadvertently by the mother. It goes without saying, of course, that the bitch should not be wearing a chain slip collar or for that matter any sort of lead in the box, otherwise there is a danger of either her or her puppies being strangled.

In order to keep the bitch and her puppies warm, lamps can be placed at a suitable distance above the whelping box. The problems here are, of course, that the heat intensity as well as the light intensity could be too much. Infrared lamps used in some cold climates are perhaps not a good idea because of the danger of overheating the bitch and her pups. If, however, you can arrange an infrared lamp above the box to use intermittently, this might perhaps avoid the problem of light intensity. Perhaps the best solution is to place the box in a spot which is well ventilated, yet warm enough to do without this electrical paraphernalia. If you really must use a heat device (not an electric blanket which could be dangerous if the dogs chewed on it!), try using a metal photoflood reflector (but with an ordinary low-wattage household bulb instead of the bright photoflood lamp in it!). Place it near the whelping box but turned away from the box so that most of the heat is projected away. This will provide a certain amount of radiant heat from the metal reflector. Another nicety which you may wish to add to the whelping box is a step, depending upon the size of your breed, that enables the mother, but not the pups, to go in and out of the box.

A WHELPING TRAY

If you are an operating room-minded person and wish to leave nothing undone to assure that your bitch will have all of the care you can offer, set up a whelping tray. This tray should contain all of the items that you foresee will be necessary for helping your bitch give birth to her pups. These items include ample quantities of absorbent cotton, well washed and ironed pieces of cloth (the heat of ironing helps to hold down bacterial contamination), a clock for timing the whelping and the time between the appearance of the afterbirths, thermometer, several rough bath towels for drying the pups, a notebook for writing down the details. . . and especially for the telephone number of your local veterinarian. . . whom you have notified several days before that his services would be required on a stand-by basis. In addition to the above items, the thoughtful owner will have also collected many other items which have suggested themselves either from previous whelping sessions or from talks with the veterinarian or other dog owners.

It is well to note that newspaper—notorious for getting ink all over children's hands and cleanly upholstered furniture—quite satisfactorily replaces cloth when dealing with birth and delivery of pups. The heat of the presses used to print newspapers cuts down the bacterial contamination in the untouched and unopened newspaper.

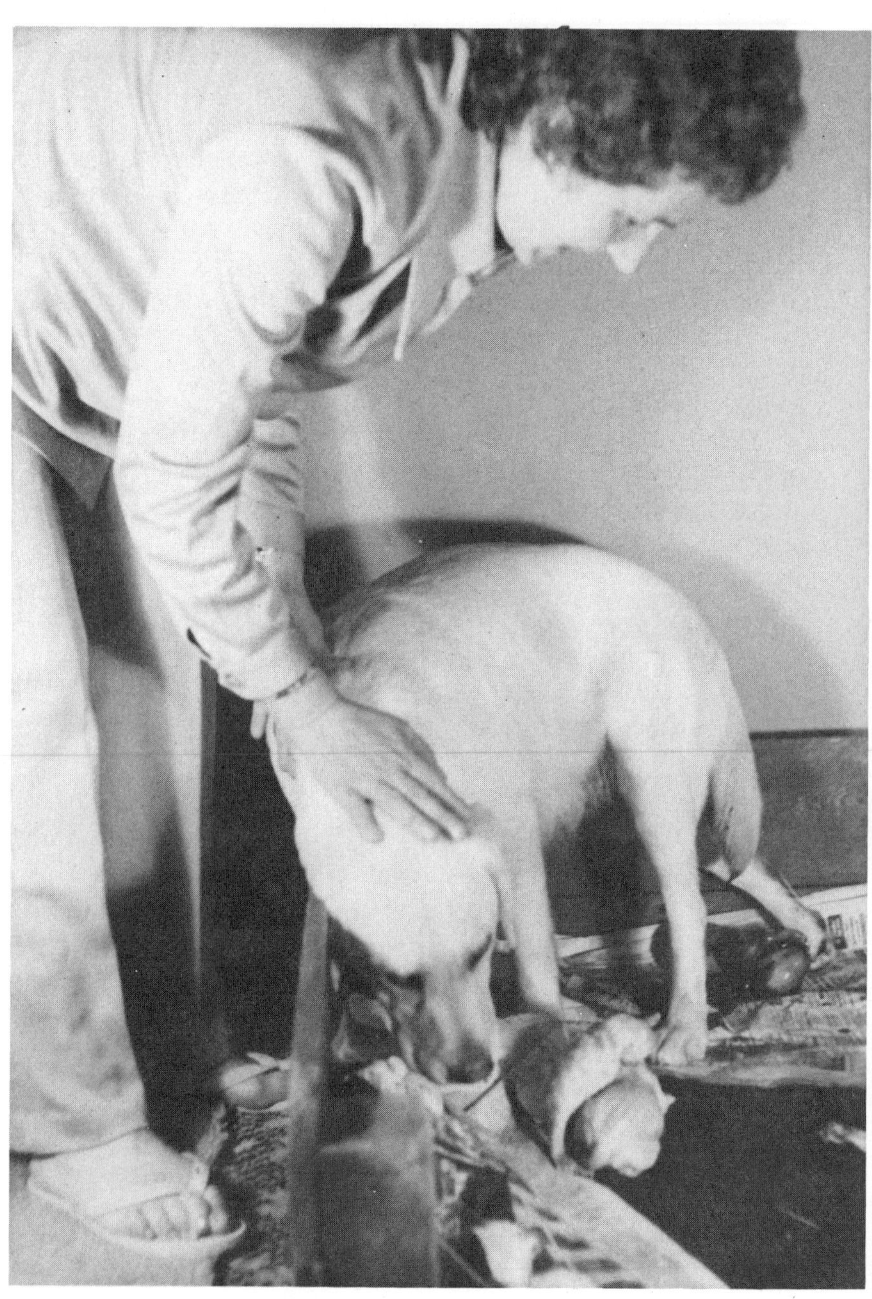

Bitches may whelp an individual pup every 15 to 30 minutes, or they can give birth to intermittent batches of pups.

CHAPTER SIX

Puppies!

MATING-WHELPING TIME

The chart accompanying this section helps you to estimate (and estimate it always is with biological mechanisms) the day you and your bitch can expect a lot of excitement and company. This chart is based upon a normal 63-gestation period.

THE FIRST TIMER

Let your veterinarian examine the new mother-to-be about three days before she is due to whelp. Milk in first timers does not appear until labor starts. Experienced bitches, however, normally have milk about four or five days before whelping.

SEQUENCE OF WHELPING EVENTS (DETAILS FOLLOW THIS LIST)

- ⋆Temperature drops twelve to twenty-four hours before the onset of labor, that is, from 101.4 °F. down to about 99 °F. (Establish the bitch's normal temperature by taking her rectal temperature daily, starting approximately two weeks prior to expected delivery date.)
- ⋆Body position tends to be stretched out, the head between forelegs, with doleful glances toward the owner.
- ⋆Restlessness, appears uncomfortable.

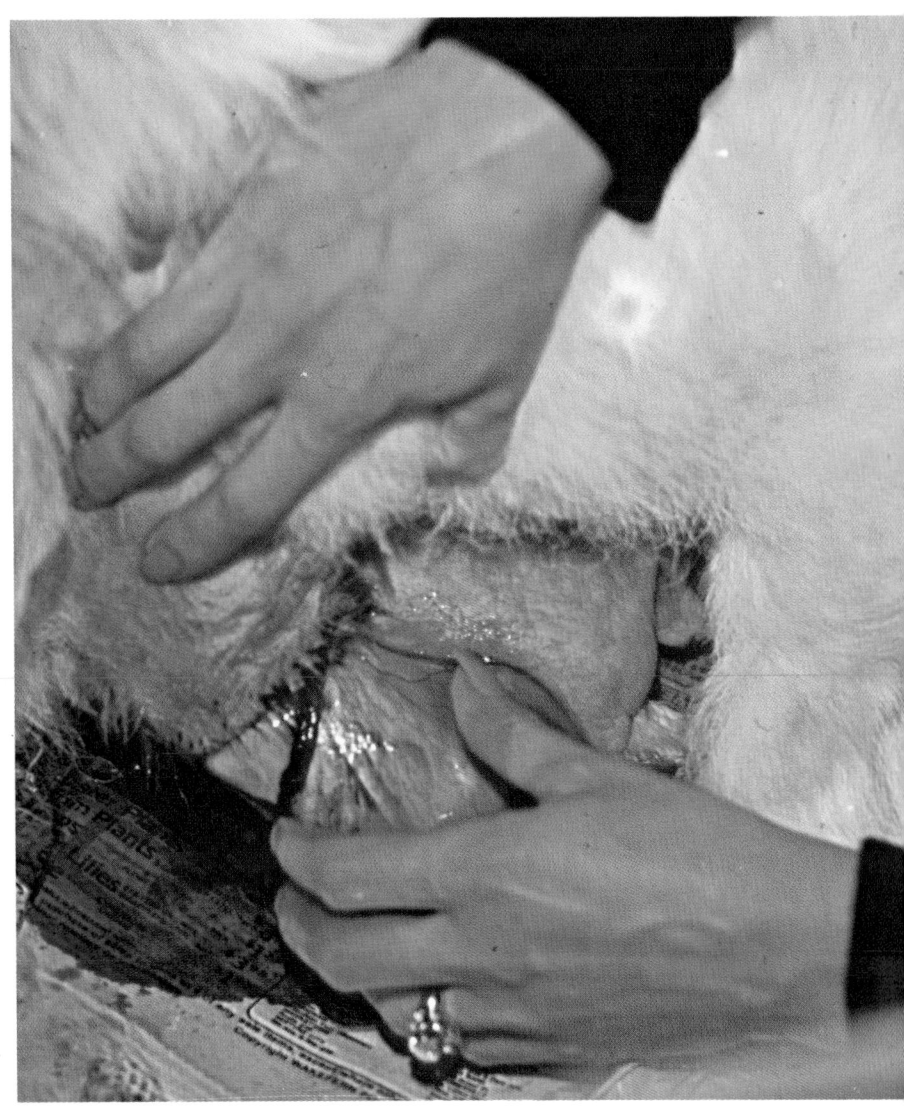

If the whelp takes an unduly long time to make his entrance into the world, you can help by grasping firmly but gently on the part that has already been delivered and easing it out of the bitch's vagina. Always pull in the direction of the dams head, not straight or toward her tail.

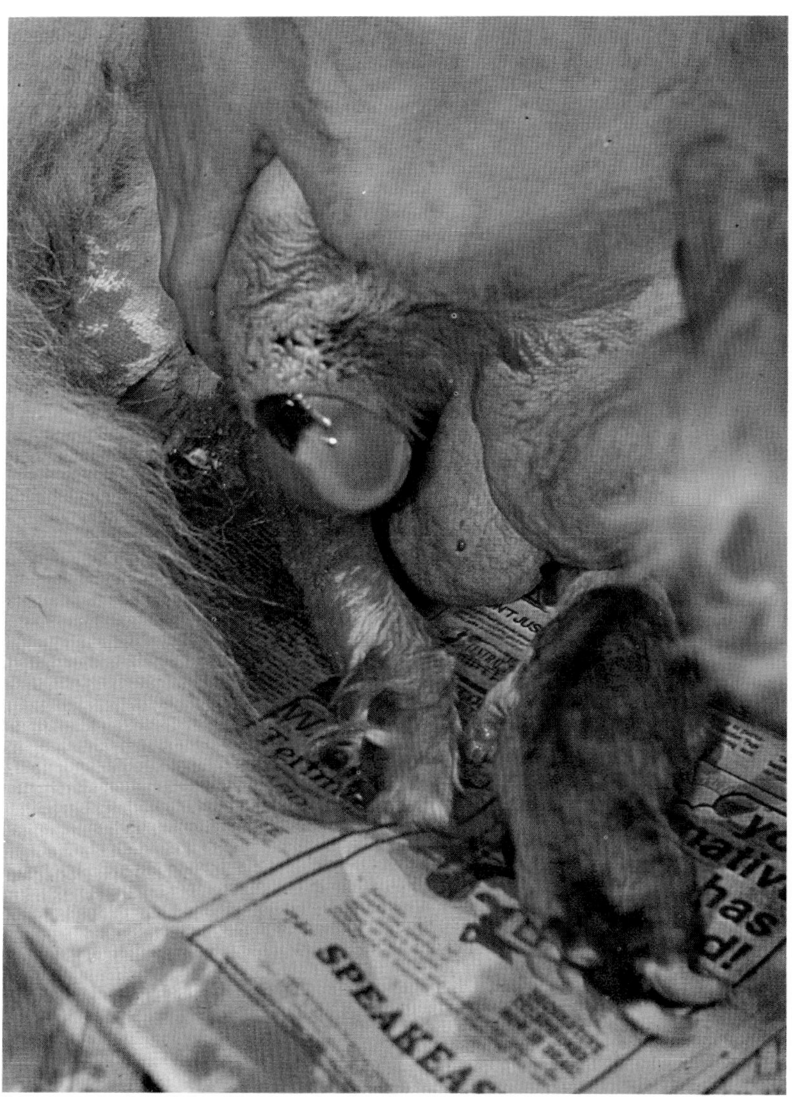

The dam has just begun delivery of another pup with the amniotic sac still intact. As the whelp is slowly forced out by labor contractions the part of the sac to deliver first appears as a small bubble from the pressure of the contractions.

Perpetual Whelping Chart

Bred—Jan.	1	2	3	4	5	6	7	8	9	10	11	12	13	14	15	16	17	18	19	20	21	22	23	24	25	26	27				28	29	30	31
Due—March	5	6	7	8	9	10	11	12	13	14	15	16	17	18	19	20	21	22	23	24	25	26	27	28	29	30	31			April	1	2	3	4
Bred—Feb.	1	2	3	4	5	6	7	8	9	10	11	12	13	14	15	16	17	18	19	20	21	22	23	24	25	26							27	28
Due—April	5	6	7	8	9	10	11	12	13	14	15	16	17	18	19	20	21	22	23	24	25	26	27	28	29	30				May			1	2
Bred—Mar.	1	2	3	4	5	6	7	8	9	10	11	12	13	14	15	16	17	18	19	20	21	22	23	24	25	26	27	28	29				30	31
Due—May	3	4	5	6	7	8	9	10	11	12	13	14	15	16	17	18	19	20	21	22	23	24	25	26	27	28	29	30	31	June			1	2
Bred—Apr.	1	2	3	4	5	6	7	8	9	10	11	12	13	14	15	16	17	18	19	20	21	22	23	24	25	26	27	28					29	30
Due—June	3	4	5	6	7	8	9	10	11	12	13	14	15	16	17	18	19	20	21	22	23	24	25	26	27	28	29	30		July			1	2
Bred—May	1	2	3	4	5	6	7	8	9	10	11	12	13	14	15	16	17	18	19	20	21	22	23	24	25	26	27	28	29				30	31
Due—July	3	4	5	6	7	8	9	10	11	12	13	14	15	16	17	18	19	20	21	22	23	24	25	26	27	28	29	30	31	August			1	2
Bred—June	1	2	3	4	5	6	7	8	9	10	11	12	13	14	15	16	17	18	19	20	21	22	23	24	25	26	27	28	29					30
Due—August	3	4	5	6	7	8	9	10	11	12	13	14	15	16	17	18	19	20	21	22	23	24	25	26	27	28	29	30	31	Sept.				1
Bred—July	1	2	3	4	5	6	7	8	9	10	11	12	13	14	15	16	17	18	19	20	21	22	23	24	25	26	27	28	29				30	31
Due—September	2	3	4	5	6	7	8	9	10	11	12	13	14	15	16	17	18	19	20	21	22	23	24	25	26	27	28	29	30	Oct.			1	2
Bred—Aug.	1	2	3	4	5	6	7	8	9	10	11	12	13	14	15	16	17	18	19	20	21	22	23	24	25	26	27	28	29				30	31
Due—October	3	4	5	6	7	8	9	10	11	12	13	14	15	16	17	18	19	20	21	22	23	24	25	26	27	28	29	30	31	Nov.			1	2
Bred—Sept.	1	2	3	4	5	6	7	8	9	10	11	12	13	14	15	16	17	18	19	20	21	22	23	24	25	26	27	28					29	30
Due—November	3	4	5	6	7	8	9	10	11	12	13	14	15	16	17	18	19	20	21	22	23	24	25	26	27	28	29	30		Dec.			1	2
Bred—Oct.	1	2	3	4	5	6	7	8	9	10	11	12	13	14	15	16	17	18	19	20	21	22	23	24	25	26	27	28	29				30	31
Due—December	3	4	5	6	7	8	9	10	11	12	13	14	15	16	17	18	19	20	21	22	23	24	25	26	27	28	29	30	31	Jan.			1	2
Bred—Nov.	1	2	3	4	5	6	7	8	9	10	11	12	13	14	15	16	17	18	19	20	21	22	23	24	25	26	27	28	29					30
Due—January	3	4	5	6	7	8	9	10	11	12	13	14	15	16	17	18	19	20	21	22	23	24	25	26	27	28	29	30	31	Feb.				1
Bred—Dec.	1	2	3	4	5	6	7	8	9	10	11	12	13	14	15	16	17	18	19	20	21	22	23	24	25	26	27				28	29	30	31
Due—February	2	3	4	5	6	7	8	9	10	11	12	13	14	15	16	17	18	19	20	21	22	23	24	25	26	27	28			March	1	2	3	4

*Concern for the area under the tail, including looking and licking.
*Perhaps she turns down food, may even appear to be somewhat ill.
*Swollen vulva.
*Clear mucoid discharge from the vulva.
*Pushes and strains with her abdomen.
*Digs and tears at bed, pants intermittently.
*Labor continues one to three hours. Call veterinarian if longer.
*The water sac (not a pup yet!) appears.
*Water sac may break spontaneously or is broken by the bitch's licking it.
*Break the membrane in the area that covers the pup's nose and hold the puppy head down to allow mucus and any fluid to drain from the nostrils and throat.
*Gently pull at the placenta by putting tension on the umbilical cord to feel if it is ready to come out. Do not pull on the puppy!
*Tie the cord with a thread or fishing line about ½-inch from the puppy and pinch or cut off the cord about one inch from the pup. Paint this umbilical stub with tincture of iodine.
*Vigorously dry the puppy and keep it warm while you clean up the afterbirth. Don't let the bitch eat the placenta and membranes as this is of little nutritional value and generally leads to digestive upset and possibly diarrhea.
*Clean up the box and line it once again with clean newspapers.
*Place the pup's mouth on a teat so it has a chance to suck its first meal.
*Have water available for the bitch.
*Let the bitch rest.
*If whelping lasts a while, let the bitch out to relieve herself as she waits for her pups, but observe her closely—she may accidentally deliver a puppy outside and it could go unnoticed.
*Account for all placentas, especially the last one (after being certain there are no more pups coming!). If you are uncertain, call a veterinarian. Many breeders routinely have the bitch and pups examined by a veterinarian within 24 hours after delivery. If undelivered pups are present he may give the bitch an injection

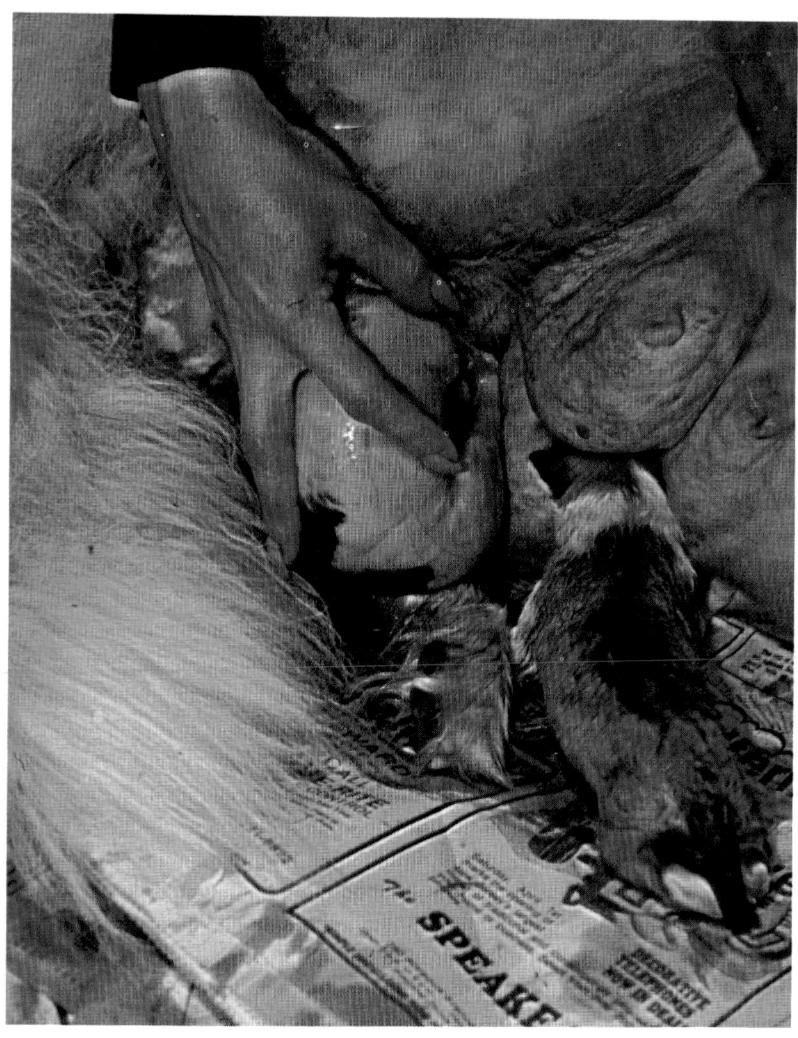

Breech presentation is almost as common as head first presentation and is not accompanied by the difficulty present with human breech births. The danger in canine breech births is that the puppy may slip back into the mother. If the placenta separates in the birth process, the puppy can no longer draw oxygen from it and may suffocate if it is not taken out quickly.

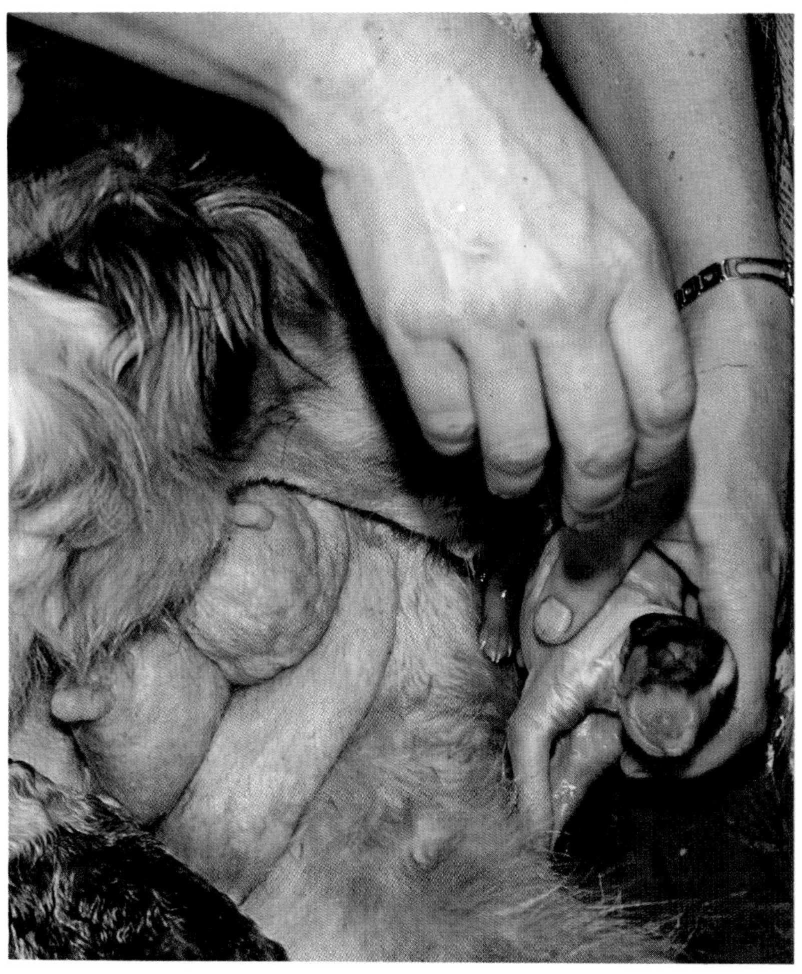

A head first delivery. The sac has already broken and the pup is ready to begin breathing, but you must still make sure mucus has been cleared from nose, mouth and throat so he does not inhale it and drown.

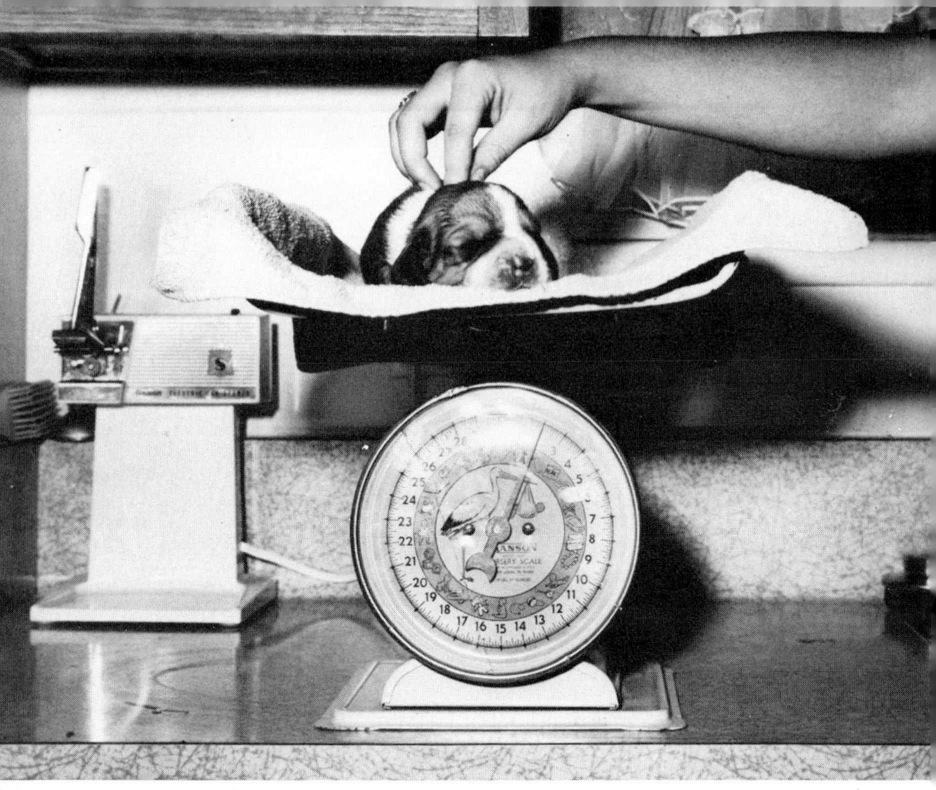

A weight gain chart for each newborn should be kept, with weigh-ins and any other observations recorded daily. This chart could be your first key signs of trouble developing in the puppies.

to stimulate uterine contractions. Your veterinarian may also want to examine each newborn pup to make certain they are free of birth defects such as cleft palate or heart anomalies.

*Be absolutely sure that all puppies are nursing adequately. The smaller or weaker puppies are likely to be pushed away by stronger littermates. Let the smaller or weaker puppies nurse once or twice a day without the interference of the rest of the litter.

*It is also advisable to keep an infant scale handy and make a weight gain chart for each pup. On this chart you should record each puppy's weight, sex and identifying characteristics. If two pups are exactly alike, you could use indelible ink to make an identifying mark on them. Weights and observations should be recorded daily as these may serve as an early indicator of possible problems.

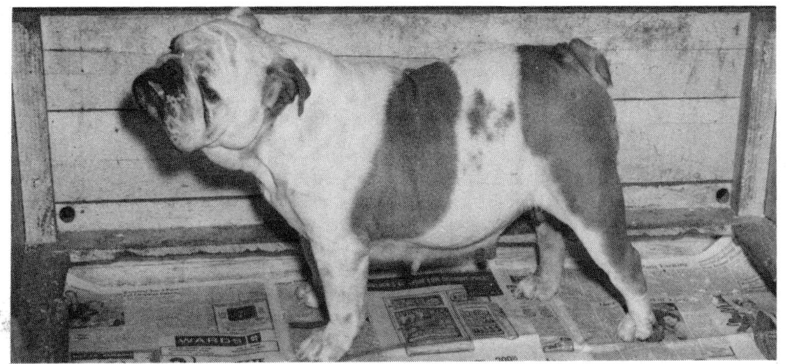

The Bulldog represents an instance where human interference in the birth process is practically a necessity. The puppies' heads and chests are so broad that they are difficult for the bitch to whelp. Her own bulk is also an obstacle to a successful birth, since it prevents her from being able to get her head close enough to her rear parts to give much assistance to the whelps.

IS INSTINCT ENOUGH?

Bitches vary in whelping behavior. The first time she whelps, a bitch does not appear to know what is going on. But do not worry, her instincts generally carry her along. If she is particularly nervous and confused, however, you can help guide her here and there through some of the procedures of giving birth.

You should recognize that some breeds of dogs have been radically changed from whatever would have been their natural condition had they not been bred for certain characteristics. For example, Bulldogs or Pekingese may need human help in whelping; these bitches with overshot or undershot jaws can easily miss the umbilical cord and bite into their own puppies instead. A bitch of one of the disproportioned breeds can be so bulky that she cannot reach her rear parts and be unable to care for her puppies.

BEING BORN

First-timers often act excitedly and distractedly, running through the house and uttering cries and noises, scratching or ripping rugs or their beds. A bitch may suddenly start having a litter just like that, as you stand and stare in amazement. Usually, too, the mother-to-be shows even more affection for her owners at this time.

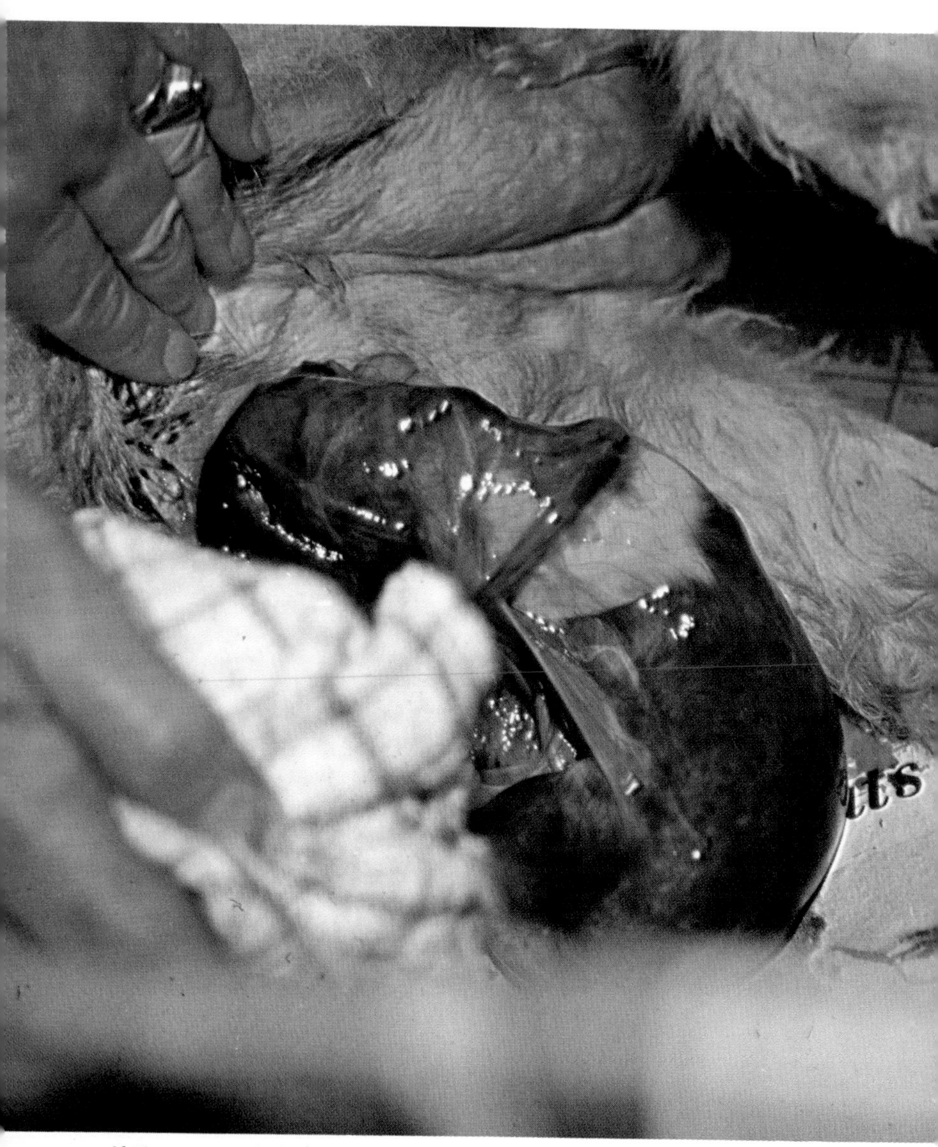

If the puppy is born with the sac still intact tear it first at the pup's head so it can begin breathing.

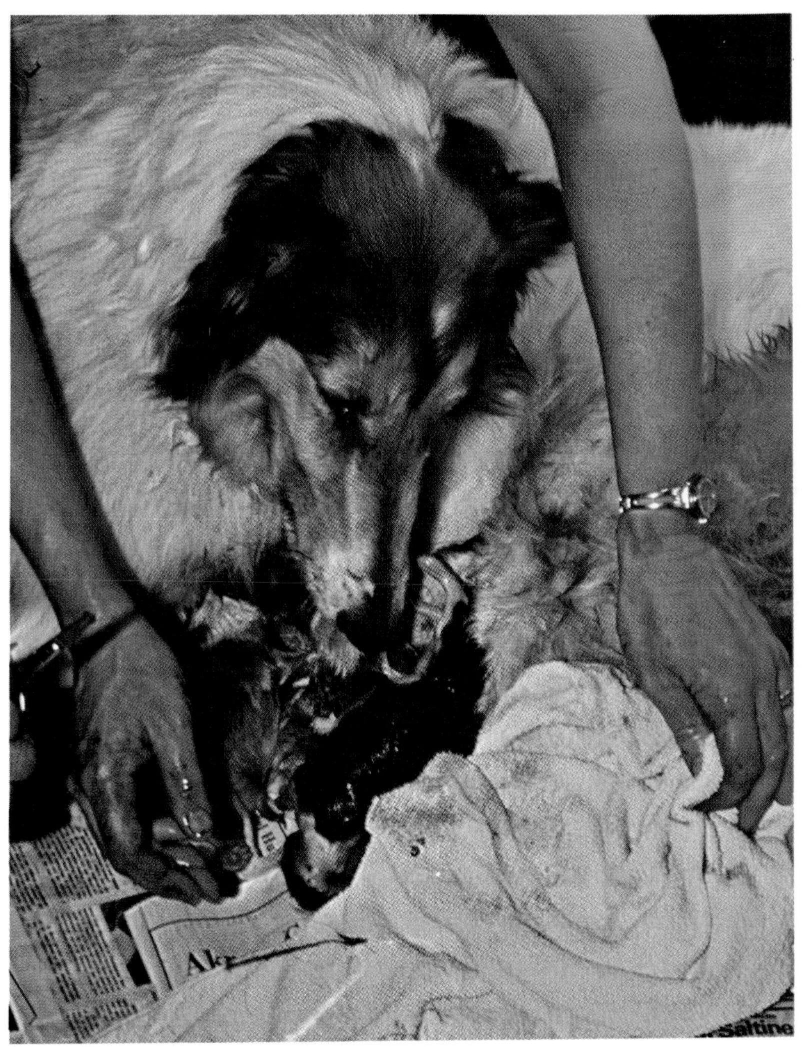

When the puppy has been delivered, help deliver the placenta by grasping the umbilical cord and pulling gently. Do not try to deliver the placenta by pulling on the pup or you may cause an umbilical hernia in the puppy.

The vagina softens, everts (or pouts) and may discharge a thick, sticky fluid several hours before delivery. Her temperature may drop to about 99 °F or one to two degrees below her normal body temperature. She may even shiver a little.

The first "official" stage of labor is dilation of the passages. The second stage includes the uterine contractions which expel the pup. The third stage involves expulsion of the placenta and membranes (usually 5 to 15 minutes after the birth of the pup, but sometimes not until the next pup is delivered).

In stage 1 as the cervix slowly dilates and the vagina and vulva relax, the bitch apprehensively watches her rear parts, gets up and down and otherwise behaves restlessly.

Bitches can whelp at 15- to 30-minute intervals, one after the other, or in spaced batches. Twelve to fourteen puppies can take several hours, a day, or even longer in some cases.

Before the onset of labor, the cervix dilates and vagina relaxes. During this stage the bitch shows much concern for her rear parts and may grow restless, getting up and down frequently.

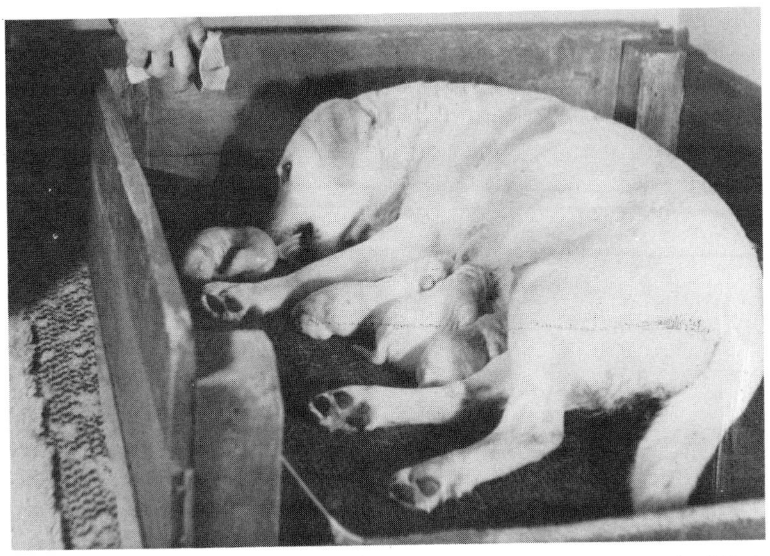

If the water sac enveloping the pup is still on when its born, the bitch usually tears it away. Being licked and nudged by its mother also stimulates the pup to find a teat and suck.

The internal pressure developed by uterine contractions forces the pups along the way to the birth canal. As the pup makes its exit—and its first entry into the world—the bitch usually licks away the fluids coming out with the pup. The water sac or membrane which envelops the pup may appear and disappear a few times until pressure or the bitch's licking ruptures it. If this sac does not rupture but is still on the pup at birth, it will probably be torn off by the bitch, who will also bite through the umbilical cord (which attaches the pup to the placenta or afterbirth). If permitted, she may instinctively eat the umbilical cord and placenta. In prehistoric times, unless a bitch ate her afterbirth predators could scent the birth and come to look for some easy prey. Fortunately, this is not a problem for your dog, so you can prevent her from following those instincts which used to favor survival of the offspring. About all she'll get from eating the afterbirth in today's world is colic, diarrhea and gastritis.

A good bitch will also instinctively lick and nudge her newborn pup, cleaning it the best way she knows how. The pup, stimulated by being licked and nosed about, is soon sucking at a teat. The

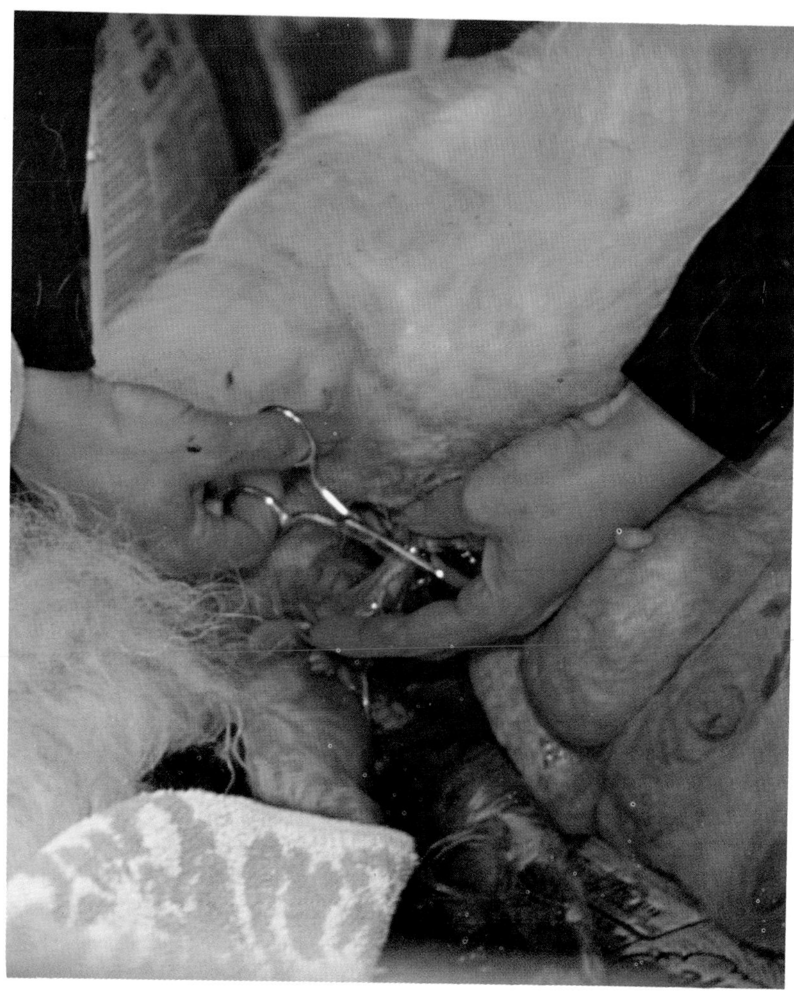

In unusual circumstances it may be necessary to snip the umbilical before the placenta is delivered. If so, use a pair of blunt end scissors to avoid injuring either the pup or the dam. But the birth process is usually long, especially when a large litter is expected and patience plays a key part. If you suspect your bitch will have a hard delivery, your veterinarian should be notified when she goes into labor.

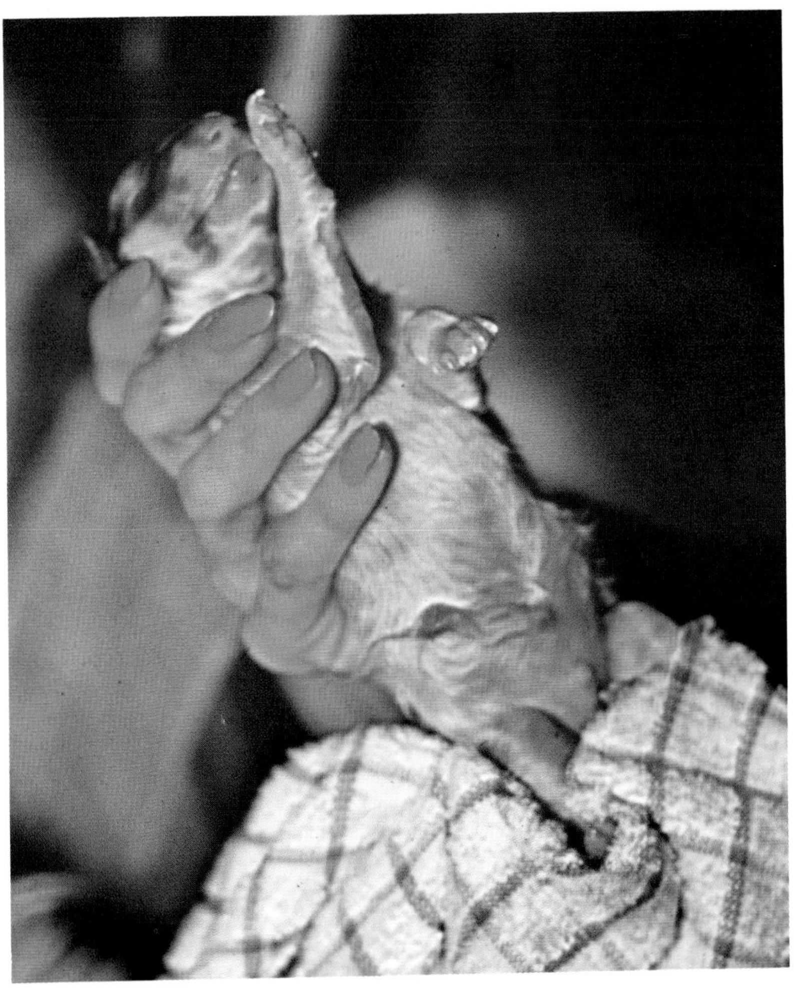

If the dam has not had time to bite through the umbilical, it should be snipped off about an inch from the puppy.

The bitch will usually sever the umbilical cord by biting through it about the same time she licks away the water sac from the newborn pup. Instinct dictates she eat the placenta and umbilical, a throwback to ancient times when the scent of these things would have led predators to an easy meal.

pup's first bowel movement also takes place about now—a sort of clearing out of the pipes. This first stool occurs after the pup sucks up some of the bitch's colostrum—a very important source of nutrition and antibodies. These antibodies aid in protecting the pup from many diseases, including distemper and hepatitis. This antibody protection is short lived, however, but usually will last until the pup is old enough to be vaccinated and produce it's own antibodies (about six to eight weeks of age). By the way, you can call your bitch a *dam* now.

The dam usually gives her pups all the food they need, at least for the first three weeks. Some breeds such as Bloodhounds or bitches with a very large litter may not produce enough milk to satisfy the demands of their litter. A hormonal deficiency could also be responsible for inadequate milk production. Therefore, it may be necessary to supplement the nursing by bottle feeding the

Supplemental feeding may be necessary for puppies in a large litter. But homemade formula should not be started before the pup has nursed its mother to collect the colostral antibodies in her milk.

pups. A variety of excellent milk substitutes are available from your veterinarian or pet store. If you don't have access to these commercially prepared formulations you could mix up your own by adding about one-fourth can of water and an egg yolk to a can of evaporated milk. The formula should be well mixed and kept refrigerated except for the portion to be fed to the pup—warm that portion to body temperature for immediate use.

This puppy's placenta was born simultaneously with it, the most desirable way for the placenta to be delivered.

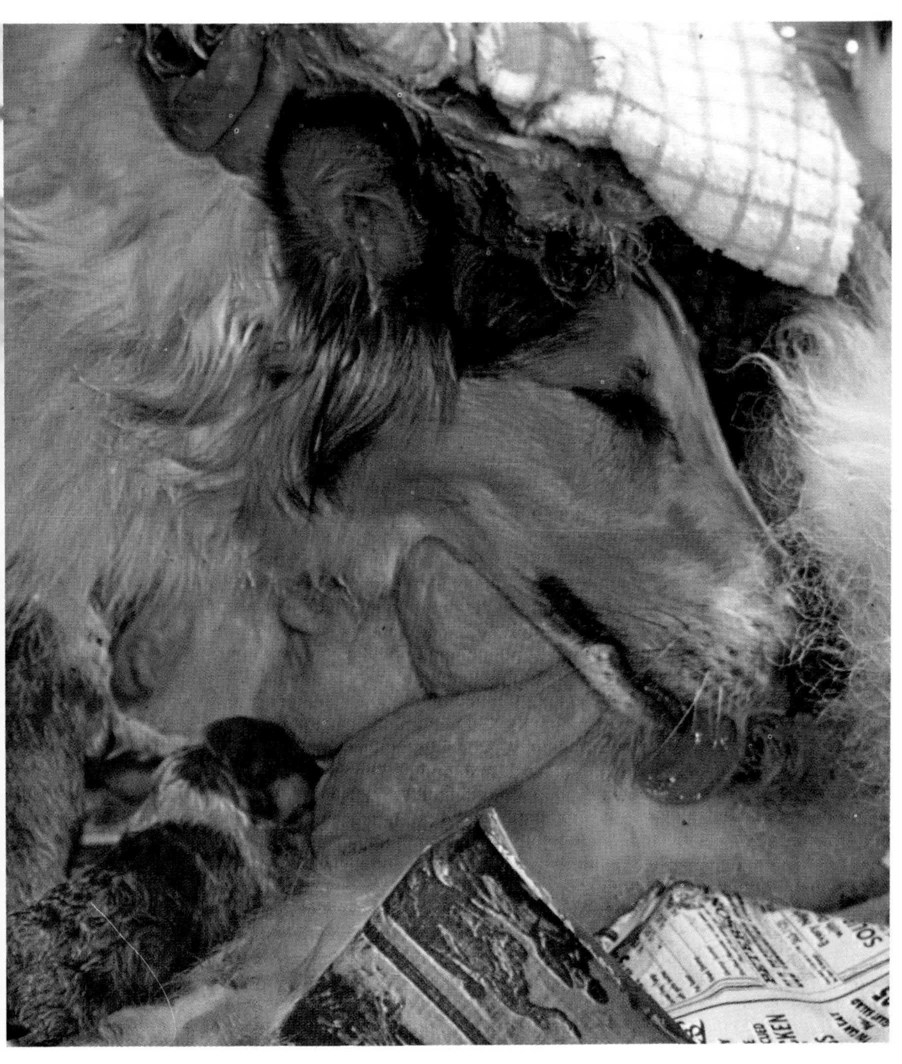

Normally, pups will be born within about 15 minutes of each other. When she is expecting the next birth, she will lick and clean the area of the vulva.

HELPING THE BITCH

First, a word about germs. Fortunately, the mother has already been exposed to many of them or has been immunized and the pups have a certain resistance from the colostrum; if not, they are in for a rough and *short* life. However, take ordinary sanitary measures such as starting out with clean materials and surroundings. You can even sterilize eating utensils and scissors after thorough washing, by boiling them at least ten minutes. This will give the new family a chance to start with only familiar germs, especially if the scissors or eating utensils have been used for other animals. Also, do not promiscuously splash strong antiseptics over mother or her puppies. They may do more harm than good. Ask your veterinarian what antiseptic, if any, to use.

If the membrane over the newborn puppies does not rupture or is not removed by the mother, do it yourself before the pup suffocates. Snip away the part of the membrane covering the pup's nose first, so it can breath.

Pull slowly and gently on the cord (if it appears that nothing is coming out any more after waiting a reasonable amount of time)

You can help your bitch by tearing the membrane covering the newborn puppy. Begin at the nose so that the puppy can start to breathe.

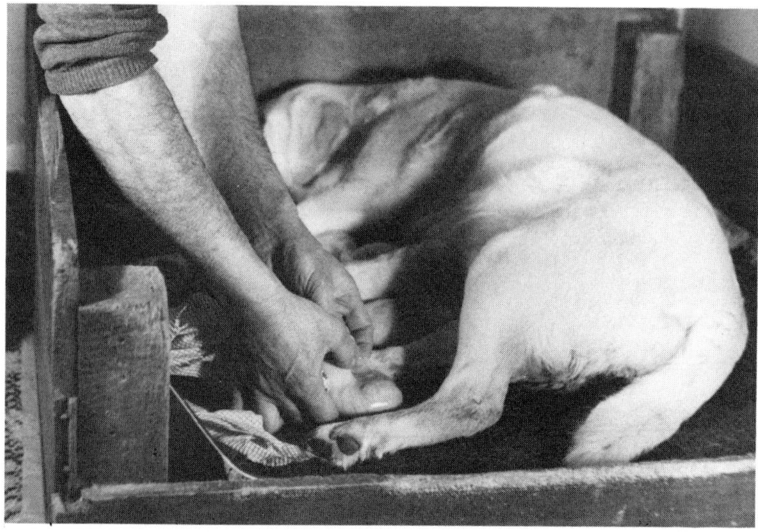

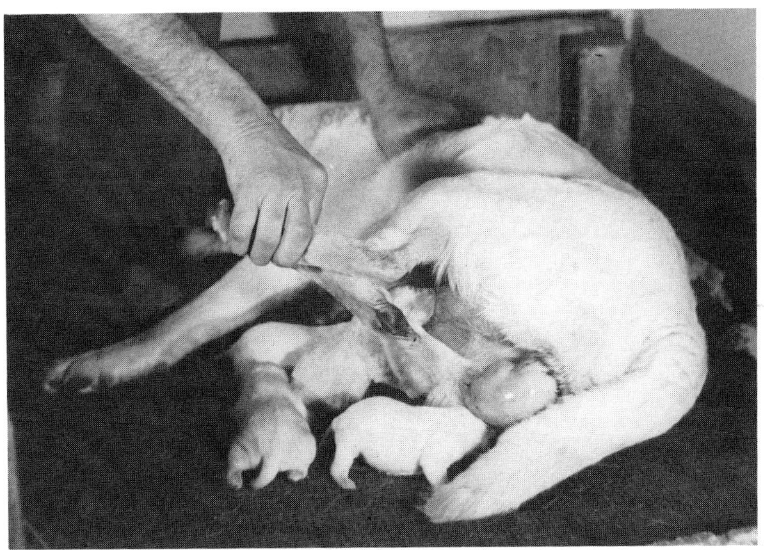

There is nothing wrong with helping your bitch deliver her puppies, providing you don't overdo it. Avoid using instruments unless there is no other alternative, then use only those that have been specifically designed for obstetrical purposes.

until a placenta comes out. Like surgeons who count gauze sponges after each operation, you, too, can keep all the placentas until all the pups are born; then you know if any are left inside the mother (unless she ate them up before you saw her do it). Retained placentas can interfere with delivery of the next puppy or predispose the dam to acquiring a very serious uterine infection. Although the placenta must eventually come out, be careful should you decide to help it along. As mentioned earlier, never pull on the pup to put traction on the placenta as you could tear the cord from the pup without leaving the desired umbilical stalk (which eventually dries up and is sloughed off). If you think you need to help, grasp the cord near the vulva of the dam with a piece of gauze and use firm but gentle traction to help release the placenta from the birth canal.

Assisting an animal in delivery is fine (that is how man survived), but "helping" your dog too much may create more problems than if you just left her alone. Instruments are dangerous, even in experienced hands, so avoid using them unless you are

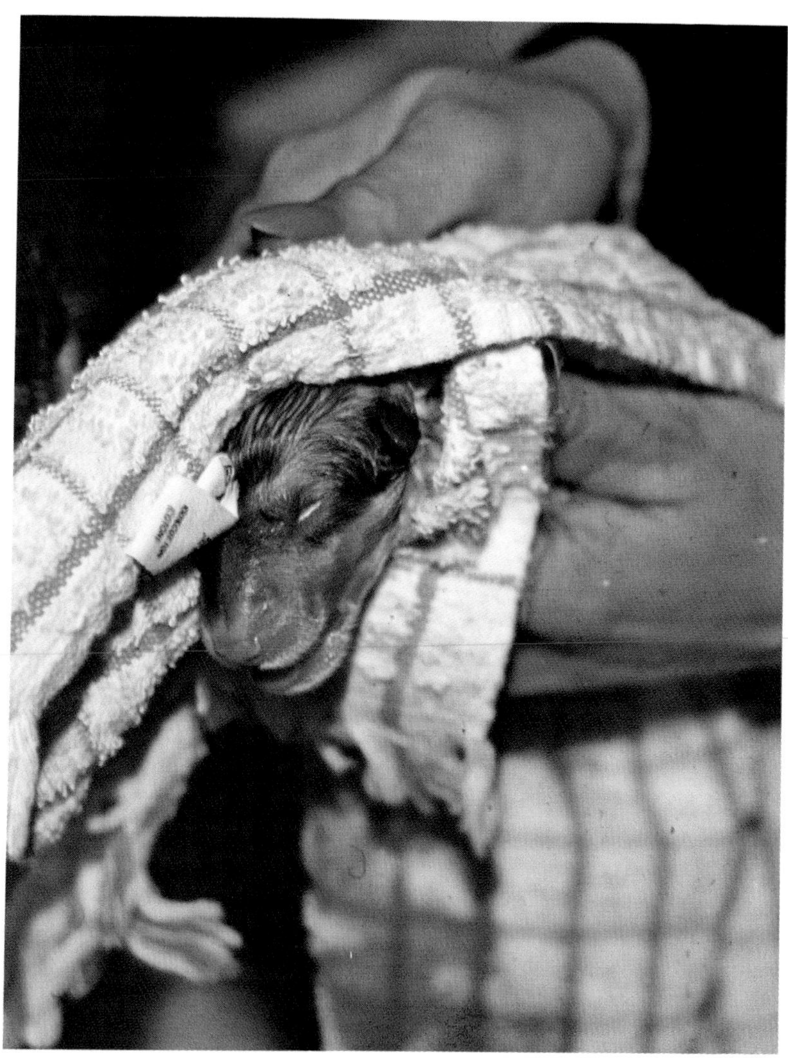

After the pup is delivered, the sac removed and the umbilical severed, rub the puppy briskly with a coarse towel until it emits several strong cries to prove it is breathing.

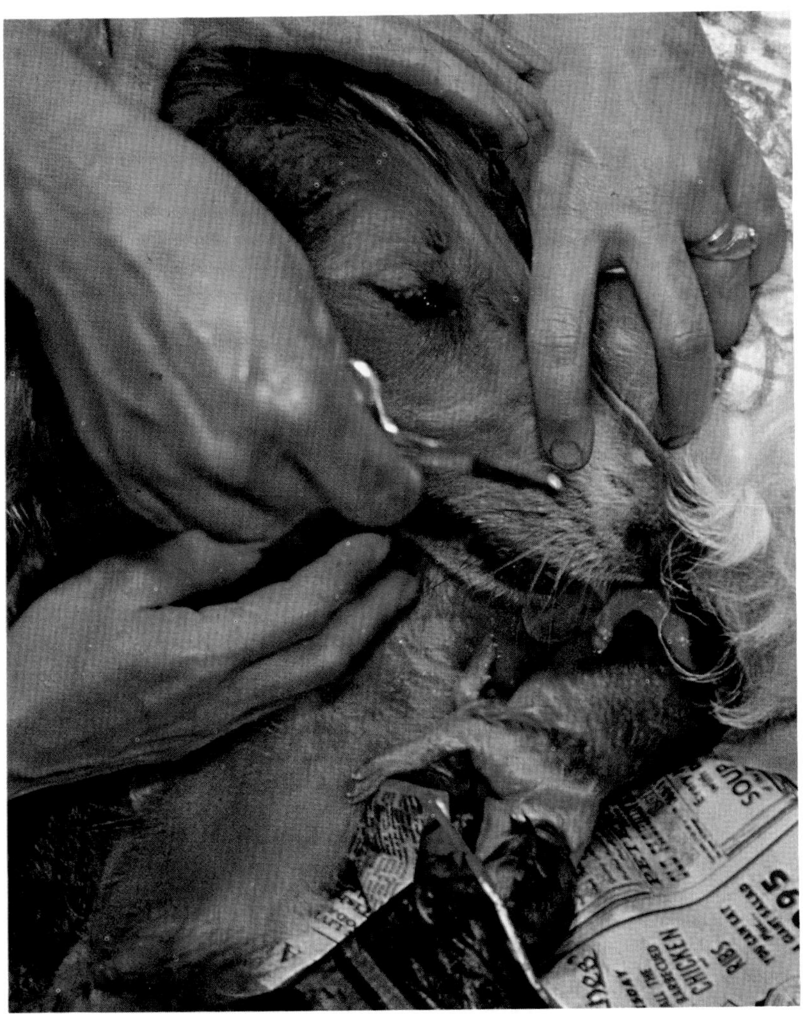

Though it is good to accustom your bitch to interference in the birth process, still many dams are good mothers, attending to all of the necessary procedures accompanying each birth. If this is the case, then allow the mother to follow her instincts. Interference may only serve to heighten the stress she is already under at such a time.

skilled in exactly what to do. If any instruments are to be placed in the vagina they should be blunt obstretical instruments designed for that purpose, anything else could damage the delicate tissues.

If the bitch has strained fruitlessly for hours and you cannot get an experienced breeder or veterinarian to come to your aid, carefully slide (do not push) a finger into the bitch's vagina. You can reduce the chances of causing infection and discomfort to the bitch if you use a lubricated surgical glove. With your finger, feel around for a tiny puppy's mouth. This feeling around may stimulate enough contractions to start the hung-up pup on its way out the birth canal. If not, you may be able to grasp a portion of the pup between your thumb and finger to provide sufficient traction to deliver the puppy. Generally, after the first pup is delivered the rest of the deliveries are uncomplicated.

If you suspect a placenta has been retained in the uterus, tell your veterinarian. By palpating the uterus, he will probably be able to determine if indeed the bitch has a retained placenta. Drugs are available that aid in the expulsion of a retained placenta.

One area where you should definitely interfere with mother nature concerns the umbilical cord. As mentioned previously, this stalk should be tied off near the pup, severed and painted with tincture of iodine. It is unwise to let the newborn pup drag the placenta around; this may lead to an umbilical hernia.

You also may need to assist in the delivery of an especially large puppy. In this case, wrap a towel around your hand for a good grip, and pull gently. Although head first is an easier delivery position, feet or tail first positions can still be delivered quite normally. If you pull, be firm but gentle and be careful that you don't twist or bend any unseen limb the wrong way.

Now that you have interfered that much, carry through by wiping the pup off with enough vigor to stimulate its dormant respiratory system, but gently enough not to injure it. Open the mouth of the newborn pup, clearing out any mucus with a cotton swab. you can then place the mouth to a teat and wait until the pup starts to suck. Or, grip the teat between the thumb and forefinger of one hand, squeeze out a drop of milk; with the other hand holding the puppy across the back, push the teat against its lower lip. The puppy should reflexively open its mouth. Now put the teat above the puppy's tongue, compressing the teat slightly and holding the pup close to the body of its mother. Sucking should start now. Hold on a few moments until the pup's suction is strong enough. A weak pup unable to hold a teat by itself should be held on until it has its fill; this may be enough to give it strength to do it alone next time.

Sucking and chomping sounds, or in and out movements of the tongue, mean the pup is not getting any (or not enough) milk. Put weak suckers on a rear teat; these teats give the most milk and are easier to suck from. A puppy tends to seek out its favorite teat; this explains a certain amount of shifting among the pups before they settle down.

CALL THE VET

Call the veterinarian, who is on a stand-by status for your bitch (remember? you called him several days ago) if whelping does not, for any reason, seem to be progressing normally. Be alert to these situations:

Once the puppy has been delivered and its respiratory system begun to function, place its mouth at a teat and hold it here until the puppy begins to suck steadily.

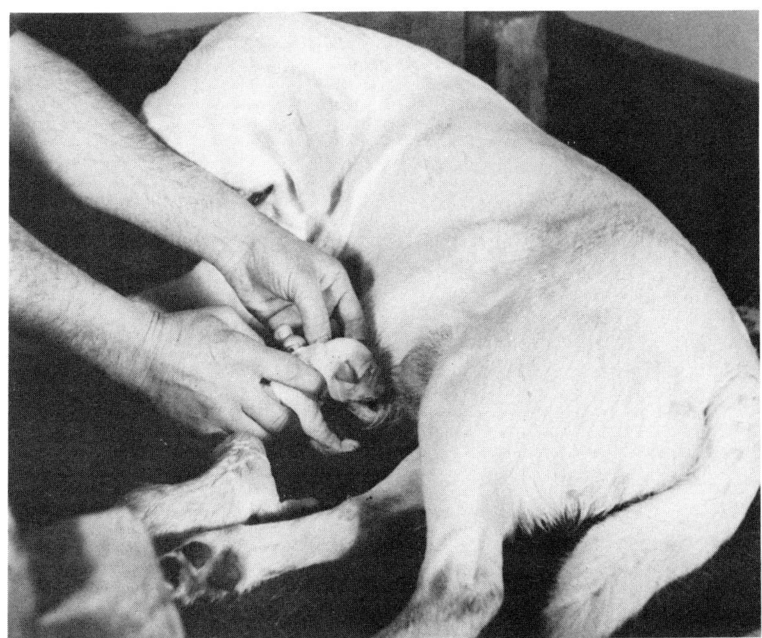

If a newborn is having trouble finding the food supply, or if you have performed most of the delivery routine up til now, go the final step and place it at a teat. You can be sure its sucking reflexes are working properly if it has curled its tongue around the teat and is pulling strongly.

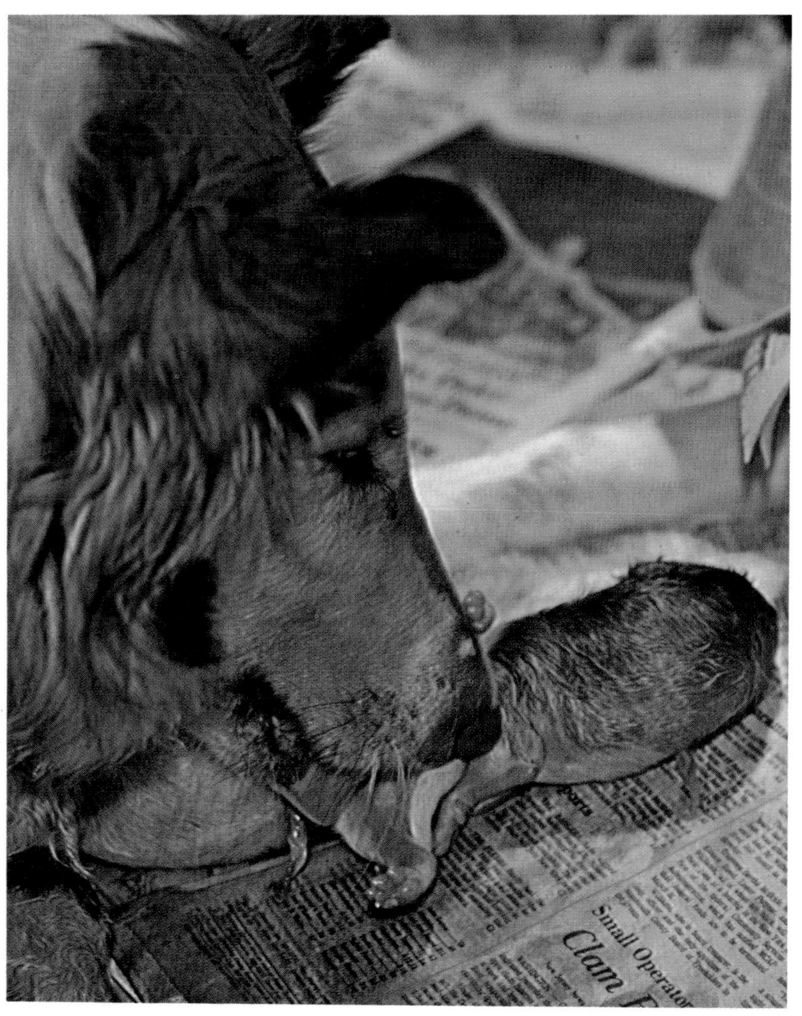

A dam that is responding to all her maternal instincts will be restless and concerned for her pups until all are sucking steadily.

1. More than three hours pass after the arrival of a pup who is not followed by a placenta or another pup.
2. The bitch appears completely exhausted before labor ceases, and labor contractions just seem to fade and become weak and non-productive.
3. Labor ceases abruptly.
4. Labor contractions have continued for two to three hours without a puppy being delivered.
5. A pup jams up in the birth canal because it is being presented in an abnormal position.
6. You are not certain that a pup is alive, or it acts differently than the others. For example, it breathes with its mouth wide open.
7. You do not know what to do, and your bitch looks like she, also, does not know what to do.

The nursing mother requires a calorie content in her diet two to three times higher than before whelping. She should be fed accordingly and not, as some believe, simply a thinned-out version of her regular diet the first few days after delivery.

Because of their broad heads and chests, Bulldog puppies present difficulties in whelping.

AFTERCARE OF THE DAM (FORMERLY THE BITCH)

Once the dam appears to have completed a normal whelping, take her out to relieve herself and then allow her to drink and eat. She may be reluctant to leave the puppies but it is advisable to encourage her. In fact, if she has not delivered all her puppies, the mild exercise may initiate additional contractions which will result in the successful delivery of any additional pups.

When the puppies are all sucking away and all looks in order, let the new mother drink small quantities of water at frequent intervals. Leave her warm and alone with her puppies after you have replaced all the soiled bedding with clean newspapers. Both the dam, and you, could stand a chance to recuperate.

Vaginal discharge, especially in the larger dogs, may continue for two to three weeks. Loose bowels may also occur for a few days after delivery. Some powdered charcoal mixed with kaolin or Kaopectate® will generally control diarrhea, but, unless a veterinarian recommends it, do not give stronger medications—- these pass through the milk and could cause harm to the pups.

Healthy newly born pups will whimper and pull themselves wobbling around, even though only minutes old, until they find a teat and settle down to steadily nurse.

Her instincts will guide the dam to lick and nose the newborns until they are actively searching for the source of nourishment.

The ability to give birth to a litter numbering as many as this Black and Tan Coonhound's is governed in part by hereditary factors.

Although the new mother is hungry, some owners feel that she should only be given milky foods or gruel every four hours for the first few days after delivery. Contrary to this belief, she requires two to three times the caloric intake now that she is nursing and should be fed accordingly. Let her drink as much water as she wants to help establish her milk supply which is now being regulated by the sucking puppies.

Three meals per day are advisable until the puppies start to be weaned. Let the new mother relieve herself often (at least four times daily) during the first week. Although she may only want to be gone a few minutes at first, encourage her to take fifteen minute breaks from the pups, gradually letting her build up her exercise. Wipe off her teats before she feeds her puppies after her walk. If the pups whimper when their mother goes out to relieve herself, try covering them up with a blanket; this usually soothes and quiets them until the dam's return.

If you are heating the whelping box (and heat should be constant, so use a thermometer), direct the heat only on the pups, not on a long-haired mother. A constant temperature of 75° to 85° F.

should be maintained during the first week after birth. Probably half the puppy deaths are due, in part, to chilling. Overheating can also be detrimental, however, as it can cause dehydration and even death. Heating pads can be very dangerous because of their potential to cause electric shock and they may overheat.

Everyone loves to see newborn pups, but try and limit visits from outside callers to very brief and distant viewings. Outsiders perturb some dams, particularly the overly maternal ones. The mother may become confused in her attempt to protect the puppies and injure or even destroy them.

ORPHANED PUPPIES

Puppies which cannot be kept with their mother lack the advantage of a nice warm body to snuggle up to; therefore, keep them warm at a constant temperature, free from drafts. During their first week of life the air temperature should be about 90° to 95° F. A pan of water close (but out of reach of the pups) to the orphans' box keeps the air from becoming too dry.

After the newborns are dried off, have taken some nourishment from their mother and are ascertained to be all right, the mother should be encouraged to go outdoors for some exercise, though she will probably resist leaving her pups at first. Watch her to make sure she does not accidentally give birth outside and abandon the puppy when she is called back in.

The Bearded Collie, one of the more recent breeds to be recognized by the American Kennel Club, makes a devoted pet, and protector of the homefront.

Opposite:
Comrade to Vikings in their ancient sagas, scholars of this breed say the form and structure of the Norwegian Elkhound evolved naturally from his pursuits and was not tampered with to fit an arbitrary mold. His well-muscled, close coupled body served well to trail and bait the huge bull elk which he still does in his native country today.

If at all possible, make sure the pup gets some colostrum from its mother during the first few hours after birth. Foster mothers or artifical formula may be nutritionally satisfying but they won't have those maternal antibodies the pup desperately needs.

When no foster mother is available, start feeding your new charges about an hour after their birth, or even before, if the puppies are obviously crying and hungry. There are several excellent milk substitutes on the market, designed specifically for growing pups. In an emergency, a pint of boiled milk containing a beaten egg yolk may be used. Cow's milk is not rich enough for puppies (dog milk has three times more protein, almost three times more fat and about two-thirds more nutritive value than cow's milk). Canned condensed milk is satisfactory for the first few days; add four teaspoonfuls of the canned product to three teaspoonfuls of boiled water.

Depending on the puppy's size, try half to one dropperful of warmed formula until the sucking reflex develops. Put only a drop of the liquid at a time on the puppy's tongue to keep fluids out of the lungs. Small swabs of absorbent cotton (without any dangling fibers which can be swallowed) can be used if droppers are not available. Dip the swab into the warm formula and then squeeze it onto the puppy's tongue. a watercolor brush (No. 6 or 8) can be soaked in the formula and then placed in the puppy's mouth to stimulate sucking. Hypodermic syringes (without needles) can be used, but do not use more pressure than needed to make the formula barely drip from the tip. Should milk accidentally get into the lungs, pneumonia can develop; therefore, bottle feeding is recommended. Doll sized bottles, complete with appropriate sized nipples, are available, specifically for the purpose of nursing orphan pups. Do not enlarge the openings in the nipple too much, because of the danger of aspiration pneumonia (or even drowning!). The same problems encountered in bottle feeding infants (clogged nipples, sucking air etc.) can occur when bottle feeding pups—you may even want to gently "burp" your orphan pup.

Persons who have adequate experience sometimes prefer to tube feed pups because of its convenience and expediency. You can feed an entire litter in five to ten minutes by tube feeding, but it must first be demonstrated to the uninitiated. By this method you can provide the pup with the exact amount of formula simply by

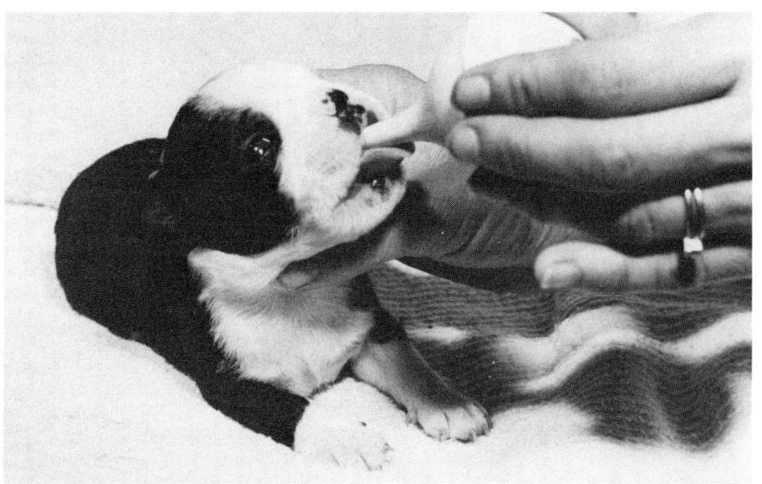

Eye droppers, needle-less hypodermic syringes and doll bottles are some of the improvised methods that can be used to feed orphaned newborn puppies. Care should be taken that the pup does not consume an excess of formula before his sucking reflex develops. It could get into his lungs and cause pneumonia.

pressing in the plunger of the formula-filled syringe. Of course the feeding tube must be expertly placed in the pup's stomach or you could make the fatal mistake of forcing formula into the lungs. If properly done, this method is especially useful for feeding very small or weak puppies with little or no sucking reflex.

During the first week of life, the orphan puppy should be fed at three to four hour intervals. During the second week you can get a little more sleep and extend the feeding intervals to every six hours. The quantity of formula varies among different sized breeds and even among individuals of the same breed. In general, a medium size breed will require approximately one-half ounce of formula per feeding, gradually increasing the amount to about two ounces when the pup is two weeks old.

You may find this hard to believe, but newborn pups cannot urinate or move their bowels without the help of the mother's licking. You can simulate this yourself by gently rubbing the puppy's stomach and genitals with a cotton pledget (small breeds) or a rough towel (for larger breeds) soaked in warm water. It's best to wipe along the abdomen toward the penis in male dogs, and, in

The trio pictured above represents the extreme ends of the size spectrum in dogdom. The Chihuahua's weight at maturity is less than six pounds, while the St. Bernard can weigh up to 125.

Opposite:
This Fox Terrier puppy portrays the alertness and inquisitiveness so typical of the Terrier nature.

female puppies, from the umbilicus down towards the tail.

Orphaned pups, deprived of their mother's colostrum, need additional protection from their surroundings. Boiling utensils the first time they are used for feeding the pups will help keep infection at bay. Some owners even continue boiling until the pups wean. Earlier immunization than the normal six weeks of age is also advisable.

When you use an eyedropper to put liquids on the tongue of the puppy, the puppy rapidly learns to curl its tongue around the tip of the dropper and suck, perhaps only after you squeeze a drop out so it gets a taste of the food. This is the same behavior a pup shows when sucking from a real teat: it wraps its tiny pink tongue around the base of the teat and swallows milk at about one-half second intervals.

A ra enous puppy sucks from the dropper too quickly, gulping it all down. In this case, take the dropper out of its mouth. If the

This compartmentalized incubator demonstrates one method of separating orphan puppies so they do not suckle each other or pile on top of one another and possibly suffocate. Orphaned pups need to be kept warmer by artificial methods than those who have their mother to cuddle next to. But whatever heating devices are used should be carefully controlled. Keep a thermometer in the box so the temperature can be regulated.

puppy keeps its mouth open and continues to suck, its tongue perhaps sticking to the roof of its mouth, correct these things at once, or the pups will swallow too much air. If the pup sucks and blows the milk up and down in the dropper, regulate the food flow so the pup does not breathe in air. If this happens, or if the puppy blows the liquid up its nostrils, take the puppy in one hand, with its neck firmly supported, and, starting in a horizontal position, shake it once downwards to bring up any liquid from the throat or out of the nose. Then you have to clean the pup's face and bib, of course.

An orphaned puppy is eating enough if it sleeps contentedly from one meal to the next without crying, and has well-formed stools without any undigested curds in them. Improperly fed puppies cry and may have greenish-yellow watery stools. Diarrhea is an especially serious problem among newborns as this can lead to dehydration. You can get a rough idea if the pup is dehydrated by lifting up a fold of skin—it should quickly return to the normal position. If the skin moves back slowly, then you know the pup is dehydrated. If a more dilute formula doesn't remedy the problem, consult your veterinarian.

Hungry pups cry for more food to fill out their flat stomachs. If this occurs, give them more formula or feed them at more frequent intervals. When properly fed, the orphan pup will sleep comfortably between meals.

Feed the puppies according to weight, not age. Feel a puppy's swollen abdomen when full; the sides should give a little when gently pressed, but if they do not and are too hard to give upon pressure, then the puppy ate too much. Put each fed puppy into a separate warm box so you know who has eaten and who has not eaten. Your veterinarian or pet shop can advise you on vitamins. It is advisable to keep orphan puppies in separate compartments to prevent suckling one another and piling up on top of each other, which could cause a possible injury or the suffocation of a weaker puppy.

FOSTER MOTHERS

Ideally, the best foster mother is a bitch who has just whelped a small litter and is about the same size as the dam of the puppies.

Results of the first outcrossings are considered mongrels until the breed stabilizes in type and desired characteristics. After several generations, it may become a recognized breed of the official kennel club.

Opposite:
The Shih Tzu's bearing and demeanor seem to reflect the awareness that he was the favorite dog of royalty at the Chinese court where the principal development of his breed took place.

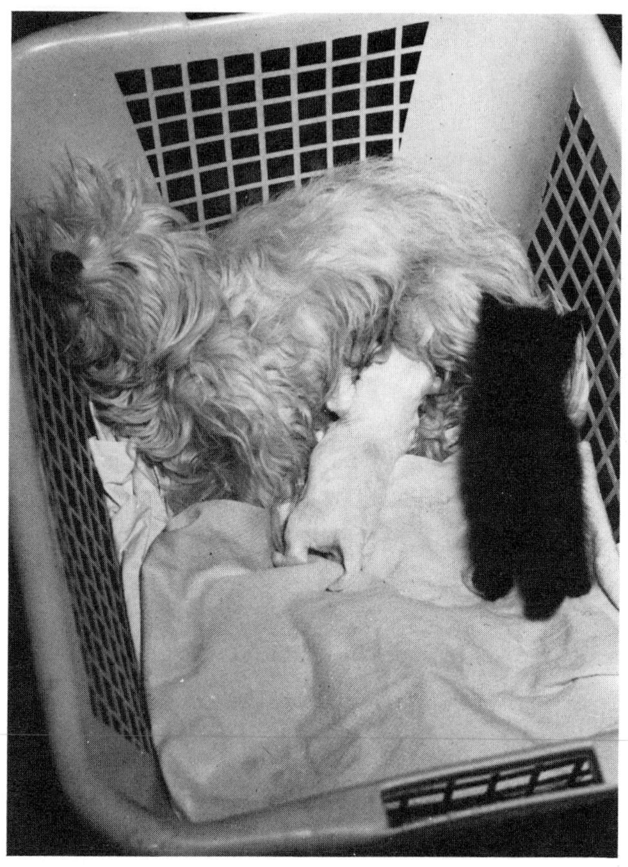

An orphaned black kitten finds that her adopted Maltese mother has room for one more. Finding foster mothers for orphaned puppies also is a desirable alternative to bottle-feeding the entire litter.

How many puppies can a dam care for? Perhaps not more than six puppies without supplementing the food. With additional food, however, and help from you, more pups can be accommodated. A foster mother's milk supply may not really be enough, but she provides love, cleanliness and warmth, too. Foster bitches can become quite possessive of their new brood.

Pups of toy breeds, or a single pup from a large breed—have been given to cat mothers for emergency care. Watch out, though, for the cat's rough tongue; if she licks puppies too much near the eyes (particularly eyes just about to open), it could act like sandpaper.

Carefully introduce the puppies into the foster mother's bed or she might kill them. Remove the foster mother from the room and bring the new puppies in, one at a time. Rub the foster mother's own puppies over the new pups. Rub some of the feces, too, if you see any, on each orphan. Space the orphans between the others. Induce the foster mother to lick them all, not just her own, by smearing a little butter on their backs. When the foster mother is brought back and she starts sniffing about, encourage all the pups to start feeding by placing each new pup at a teat. Give the bitch one of her puppies to lick, then one of the new ones; if she licks it she will most likely keep it. Or, another way, you can introduce the pups singly to the mother, without removing her.

If the foster mother growls at the new pup and refuses it, try taking all puppies away, including several of the bitch's own; keep them together for awhile in a box so they all acquire the real pups' odor, then give them back to the bitch. Hopefully, the real ones will not take on the strangers' odor!

Before leaving them all alone, satisfy yourself that the foster mother is treating all as her own litter.

THE UNWANTED

Some puppies are usually destroyed. Some owners, of course, would not destroy their pups based upon the standards of other owners who are avid breeders. A pup bearing the wrong color or coat—that is, one not allowed by the breed standard—may be done away with, as well as the seriously deformed ones. A veterinarian can put unwanted pups "to sleep" humanely or assist in finding suitable homes for the pups that are not malformed enough to make life miserable for themselves or their owners.

HEAT AND BEAT

Puppy temperature is approximately 100 to 102°F. Pulse rate is around 160 to 200 a minute, depending upon breed. Respiration rate is about 20 to 30 breaths every minute. Of these three measures of puppy life, the pulse or heart beat is most different from that of the adult dog; the adult range is 100 to perhaps 130

The standard for the Norwich Terrier allows for the ears to be either prick or drop. If they are pricked they should be small, pointed and erect; if they are dropped they should be small with the break occuring just above the skull line, and the tip of the ear not extending below the outer corner of the eye, and the front edge of the ear lying close to the cheek.

Bobbing the tail of the Old English Sheepdog is believed to date back to an eighteenth century method used to mark the dog as a drover's dog in driving sheep or cattle into the metropolis. Dogs employed this way were exempt from taxation.

beats a minute. A slow pulse in a newborn puppy could be a bad sign.

Remember, as previously stated, warmth is a prime factor in puppy survival, but make sure that you do not stifle it with uncontrolled heating devices. Keep a thermometer in the puppy box (out of harm's way). Orphan pups need somewhat greater warmth in the box for the first week than do pups who can snuggle up against their mother; some breeders consider 95 °F. or so good for these motherless ones. Other pups, however, those with their mothers, need only about 75 °F.

Puppies who are mismarked according to their breed standard are fair candidates for destruction by some breeders. Other breeders will sell them for pets only on the condition they are never shown.

The English Cocker Spaniel was drawn from the same litter as Springer Spaniels with separation of the two based only on the larger size of the latter. The two were routinely interbred even after separate classes for each were established. It was not until an extensive pedigree search of the breed was conducted by Mrs. Geraldine Dodge, that the strains were historically separated.

The pulse can be taken inside the thigh of the hindleg (from the femoral artery) of an adult or large pup. If you cannot find the artery which carries the beat in the hindleg, then feel the heart beat on the left side of the chest about the level of the elbow.

The young of any breed, raised together usually manage to refute theories of natural enmity. Puppies and kittens living together peacefully is not an unusual happening. Care should be taken to note their separate preferences and needs as they become older. The same products for ridding external parasites, for instance, should not be used on both as cats do more self-grooming and ingest a great deal more of powders or sprays meant for external use only than do dogs.

A Bulldog puppy comes by its spread eagle posture naturally because of its structure.

CHAPTER SEVEN

What's Wrong Again?

Events which are complications in one breed are normal occurrences in other breeds. For example, an undelivered pup blocks all the pups backed up behind it and can delay their birth long enough for them to die. A bitch—especially an old one—with a small litter tends to throw an oversized pup more often than other bitches, and such an extra-large pup can obstruct the birth canal. An occasional large pup is especially liable to appear, too, when a breed has been "bred down" in size too hastily; a genetic "throw back" is thus born.

Bulldogs, Pekingese and other breeds with large, broad heads invite trouble, and your veterinarian will be anticipating the potential necessity of a Caesarean section. Because of their bulkiness, the dams have difficulty reaching their rear parts to assist in delivering the pups. And the large heads of the puppies sometimes prevent them from being delivered normally.

When a whelp seems to be stuck and hung up in the birth canal, and gentle traction does not seem to help, then you must decide whether it warrants your contacting your veterinarian. Nevertheless, you still have to act, in many cases, until that help is available.

Scrub your hands and under your nails well, trim any rough edges from your nails, and rub in an antiseptic lotion. Gently insert a finger into the vagina and hook it over the neck of the pup. Steadily pull it down and out, thus lending the bitch a little extra help when she needs it.

The following descriptions and manual manipulation notes for correcting problem presentations are meant to instruct generally

Pekingese puppies, like all pups, should be fed four to six times a day, one ounce of food per pound of dog. Maximum weight of a Peke at maturity is 14 pounds, so the amount fed will vary according to the size of the individual. The Pekes' needle-like teeth are for biting, not chewing, so any food should be cut into very small pieces.

These Westie pups exhibit the friendliness and readiness for a romp that characterize the breed even through adulthood.

rather than encourage the owner to use them. Although an experienced person may do a good job, these manipulations should only be used by the owner when the veterinarian is not immediately available, when there is no doubt that the bitch is in dire distress (but remember that a certain amount of stress is normal), and when all else has failed to alleviate the bitch's dystocia (i.e. difficulty in delivery).

Delayed Head Presentation: Head born, back of pup uppermost. If the rest is not forthcoming in a few seconds, tear membrane open (gently!) at the mouth so the pup can breath. It will still have some trouble breathing because its lungs are still being compressed further back up the birth canal. Grasp the pup by the nape, pull the head down and forward, between the bitch's hind legs in the direction of her nose. If this does not work at once, work the head first to one side then to the other to unwedge the shoulders. If you happen to see a limb stick out, urge it forward and out, in the direction of the bitch's tail to release one shoulder from the pelvic brim (the bony orifice over which the pup passes). Do likewise with the other shoulder to unwedge it. When you have worked the wedge-like shoulders past the brim, do not pull the pup out in the direction of the bitch's tail but rather around and forward as explained above. Twist slightly to deliver.

Another way, when the shoulders are out and the pup is quite large, is to grip (using a towel because pups are slippery) the (almost) newborn pup by whatever is already out, steadily applying a gentle pull. The bitch's uterine contractions should finish the job.

Breech Presentation: This is perhaps as common as the head first presentation. Hind legs and tail appear. Water sac intact. Hold on to the feet when they first appear to keep them from slipping back into the bitch. Once the placenta separates, the puppy is no longer getting its blood oxygenated from the mother's blood and you are working against time. Feet slip out of your grasp easily, and they are delicate, so do not pinch, just hold firmly. However, if the feet elude you and slip back into the birth canal out of sight, the pup may suffocate or drown (if the water sac breaks or the placenta loosens from the uterus) before you get hold of them again. You have a minute or so to get the newborn pup breathing. It may help to stand the bitch on her feet (while supporting the pup with your hand, placed under the bitch's abdomen), and have an assistant (using a cloth for a non-slip holding surface) grasp whatever part of the pup is out, with steady traction of the feet. As more pup is born, grasp with the other hand the next section of the pup without releasing what you already have in hand, gradually pulling down and forward. See the section in this book on resuscitation; it may be needed for this pup if the placenta has separated and it has been deprived of oxygen too long.

Neck Presentation: Head bent with neck at pelvic brim. Crown and nose jammed in the brim opening. Attempt to push the pup back a bit so as to free its nose by lifting its chin over the brim of the pelvis.

Limb Presentation: Pull the limb forward to unwedge the shoulder (if it is a forelimb which is sticking out) on that side, then do likewise for the other side. Twist and pull slightly toward the

Uterine interia—when the bitch strains for hours without delivering a pup, or goes through all the motions of labor without actually having contractions—can cause the death of the pups or even her own. The condition can be treated medically, or Caesarean section may be called for.

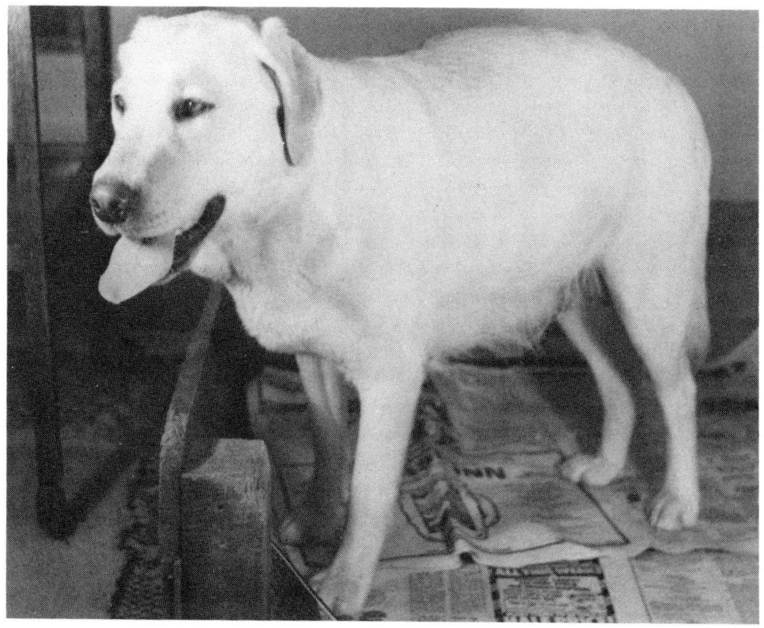

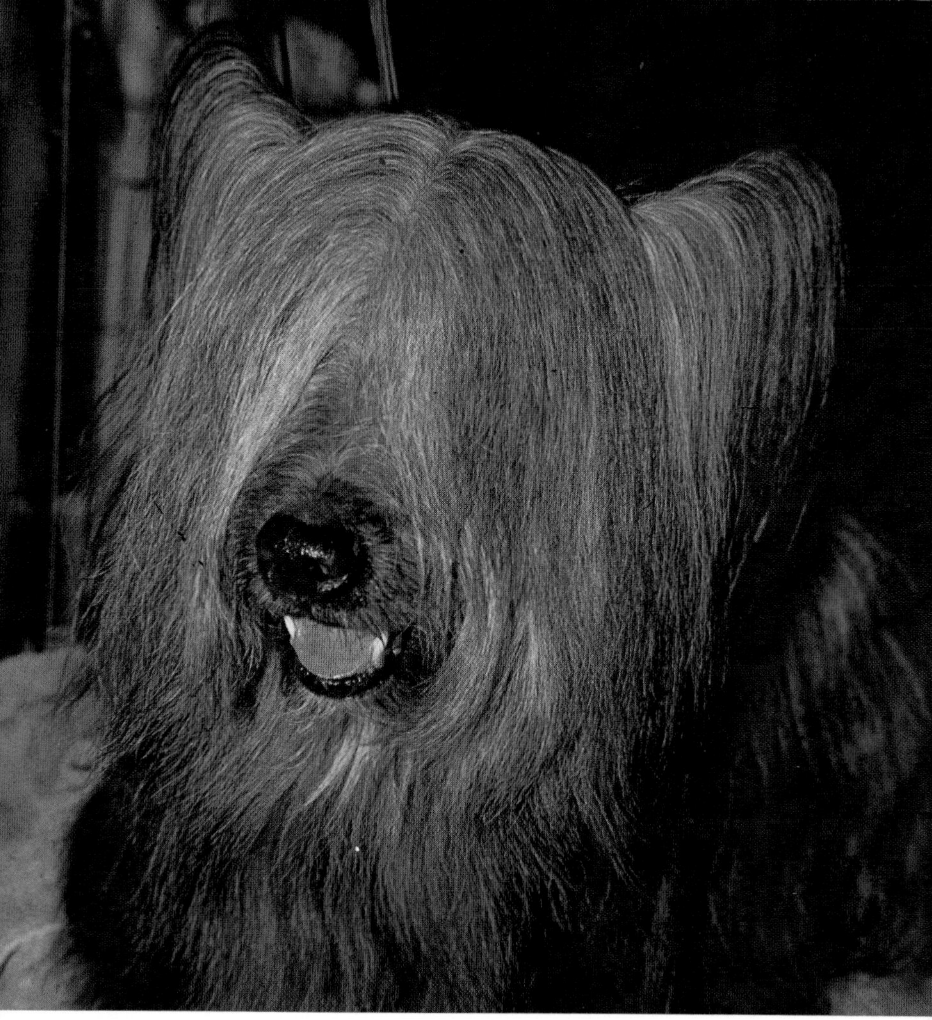

The Skye Terrier developed, as its name implies, on the craggy Scottish Isle of Skye and was used by native inhabitants to keep down the fox, badger, and otter population, among other creatures island residents considered destructive. Its long hair covering the eyes, legs and feet alike afforded it valuable protection in confrontations with its quarry.

Opposite:
Early spring or late winter is usually the most desirable time for breeding since puppies can be born and brought through the most critical first weeks of life in temperate spring or early summer weather. Still, the offspring from late fall matings may be more saleable because of their arrival near the Christmas season.

bitch's nose (not straight out behind the base of the tail, unless you are attempting to disengage a wedged shoulder, as described above).

Abdomen-up Presentation: If a whelp appears upside down, its abdomen turned up, attempt to turn it gently so that its back is up, if possible. If not, it may still come out all right.

When helping the bitch with one of her pups whose presentation is troublesome, wait about five or ten minutes if the pup appears to be stillborn; the bitch may have another contraction which will let you pull the pup out more easily than if you just pulled.

THE DECISION

If you cannot loosen a blockage caused by two pups in the birth canal to get them out before they suffocate or injure the bitch, and if a veterinarian is not available or you cannot get to him with bitch and pups, and your bitch is obviously suffering (as you certainly are, too), than use your own discretion in sacrificing one of the blocking pups. Remember, if these do not come out, the remaining pups will die, and the mother may also perish. Calm decisions obtained through good judgment are the tools most valuable to anyone.

FETAL RETENTION

Have all the pups been born? A moment or so after one pup is born, the next one in line may be palpable in a horn of the uterus, but if you wait too long to feel for the pup, the uterus may meanwhile contract and feel hard itself (just like a pup). If a bitch who is taken out to do her duties just following the birth of pups keeps straining as if constipated, have the veterinarian see her at once. She may be trying to expel a pup. The longer a dead pup is retained, unborn, the more danger is involved for the bitch.

PELVIC DEFECTS

Although you know that broadheaded breeds may be abnormal enough to have some problems in being born, you should also know beforehand whether your bitch has any hereditary or acquired pelvic deformations. Hopefully, she was seen by a veterinarian before being mated. Certain pelvic conditions would alert you and your veterinarian that a Caesarean section was going to be needed to bring the puppies into the world.

INERTIA

If the water sac ruptures, or the bitch rips up paper, paws at the rug, or pants. . . *without* having any visible contractions, she may be suffering from uterine inertia. Othertimes the bitch may strain for two or three hours without producing a pup. If she continues to strain, tiring herself to the point of exhaustion, then the energy she needs for uterine contractions may become depleted. These forms of uterine inertia can be medically treated. If treatment with the appropriate drugs fails to give productive results then a Caesarean section is indicated—trust your veterinarian's judgment as to which procedure is best. Don't wait until your bitch is exhausted before calling your veterinarian, either. Uterine inertia is a serious problem which could result in the death of the pups or even the bitch; if it occurs *day or night*, call your veterinarian.

ABSORPTION OF FETUSES

Although canine abortions do occur, perhaps more commonly the fetuses are absorbed. Occasionally a dead and incompletely absorbed fetus is expelled during the delivery of a large litter; more commonly, however, the absorbed fetus goes unnoticed unless metritis (uterine infection) or other complications occur.

PLACENTAL RETENTION

Have all of the placentas been delivered? The last placenta, if any, is usually the one to be retained. . . no one thinks of looking for it, either, in all of the excitement of seeing the new arrivals. Settle any doubts you have by calling the veterinarian, who can give medication to make the uterus contract so it can expel this last placenta. Retained placentas lead to infection and high temperature, just as do retained pups. You may have to hand-care for a bitch's healthy offspring (following delayed expulsion or removal of her retained placenta or pup) until her temperature drops down to normal and any infection clears up. In such a case, refer to the sections on the orphan puppy in this book.

This young St. Bernard appears to be watching out for his smaller chum of approximately the same age.

One of the most distinctive features of the Siberian Husky is the variety of markings and coat color evidenced by the difference between this Husky mother and her pup. Brown or blue eyes conform to the standard.

HERNIA

Congenital hernia may occur in any breed. It may be acquired or inherited by the bitch and could involve either or both horns of the pregnant uterus. If this should occur, surgery would be required at once to save the life of the bitch. Because this may be an inherited defect, it is questionable if she should be used for breeding purposes. Despite the cause of the hernia, if it is of any significant size, it should be repaired at a relatively young age and certainly prior to breeding.

REVIVING PUPPIES—Methods 1 to 8

Immediate first aid may save some of the pups who do not start breathing spontaneously at birth. The following are ways of stimulating breathing, making the puppy take its first gasp when it does not seem forthcoming of itself. All of the following methods, of course, are not necessary for each pup, although you may have to try them all until you find one that not only works but that you can do adequately and comfortably.

Method 1. Lift the pup with both hands, supports its neck and rapidly swing it downward in an arc between your legs so that mucus or liquid will be expelled from its airway by centrifugal force. Do not open the mouth.

Method 2. With a dry cotton swab, wipe out the throat and pharynx to remove any mucus obstructing the upper airway and at the same time stimulate a respiratory gasp.

Method 3. Rub the hair on the nape of the neck vigorously, backwards and forwards.

Method 4. With fingers and thumb, compress the rib cage every half to full second or so to stimulate the heart and lungs.

Method 5. Rub the pup *very vigorously* with a very warm towel.

Method 6. Hold the puppy head downward to let abdominal contents push on the diaphragm and thus the lungs, then turn the pup head up so that the abdominal contents drop back again, creating a vacuum in the chest; the next headstand releases the vacuum and pulls air into the lungs. Continue this head-up-head-down motion about twenty times within about a minute.

Doberman experts maintain that the Doberman Pinscher's primary use as a guard dog does not prevent it from being a valuable family dog and companion, the emphasis being on protection of the family. They do advise, however, that special care be taken to introduce the Doberman to its family properly. Teach it whom it is to protect and what it is to protect against, this latter ideally being *not* family friends and neighbors.

Method 7. Stand the pup up to its neck in cold water, then switch it to very warm water.

Method 8. Toss (really gently drop) the lifeless pup from one hand into the other to make it gasp.

MOUTH-TO-MOUTH ASPIRATION

To remove mucus and fluid from blocked airways, tilt your head back and hold the pup's head down with its nose and mouth covered by your own mouth. Give a strong suck, then spit out the liquid you aspirate. Some owners say that this aspirated fluid is

These Saluki hounds seem to have fixed their gaze on some distant object that may at any moment become fair game for a chase. One of the oldest known breeds of domesticated dog dating back to the time of Alexander the Great, the Saluki is a sight hound valued for his tremendous speed. Historically, the Moslems considered him sacred, the Arabs used him to bring down the fleet-footed gazelle, and the Algerians trained him for wild boar hunts. England used the dog to course hares, while jackals and foxes are believed to have been among its quarry through the decades as well.

Recently recognized by the American Kennel Club, the Bearded Collie's color varies in shades from buff and deeper brown through slate gray to almost black, usually mixed with white.

Pups that have just been taken from their dam via Caesarean section should not be given to her to nurse until she has regained full consciousness. Then introduce them to her one at a time, making sure she has accepted them before leaving them alone.

sweetish and not too unpleasant. . . and this is, by the way, how an Eskimo grandmother clears out the nose of her grandbabies, if that is any consolation to you.

MOUTH-TO-MOUTH RESUSCITATION

The opposite of mouth-to-mouth aspiration is mouth-to-mouth resuscitation. It is tricky because you cannot always blow air into the lungs without getting it into the stomach, and air in the stomach inhibits normal breathing.

You will probably find that a combination of these methods may be necessary to stimulate breathing in a puppy that does not breathe spontaneously on being born. Do not be hasty to give up. Although permanent brain damage will occur with prolonged oxygen deprivation, newborn puppies appear quite resistant to this as compared to older pups or adult dogs. Your most desperate attempts will at times be extremely rewarding. Remember, giving up will certainly be fatal.

After a weak puppy has started to breathe, you may administer oxygen for an added boost. If you have access to an oxygen tank, regulate the oxygen flow to about two liters per minute. An inverted funnel makes a convenient facemask. Or, put the puppy in a plastic bag, then run oxygen through the bag (leaving an outlet for the used gases to escape) until the pup's bluish or whitish tinge changes to pink or red, and breathing seems to have brought on normal strength and activity. Plastic bags designed specifically for this purpose are commercially available and are commonly used on puppies that have been delivered by Caesarean section.

ECLAMPSIA

Eclampsia, also known as milk fever, puerperal tetany, post parturient paresis and nursing fits, is a metabolic disease characterized by rapid breathing, restlessness, nervousness and whining. Later in the course of the disease the bitch may stagger, develop stiff limbs and an elevated body temperature. Severely affected bitches are unable to rise and lie there with extended legs, excessive salivation, chomping movements of the mouth, clonic and tonic spasms, congested mucous membranes, labored respiration and rapid pulse. If left untreated eclampsia can lead to convulsions and death.

Eclampsia is seen in bitches most commonly during the first three weeks of lactation, but may be seen prior to, during or up to six weeks after parturition (delivery). It is caused by too low a serum calcium level due to malfunction of the pituitary gland. It occurs most commonly in the small or medium size breeds.

Eclampsia is an emergency situation and requires immediate treatment. If a calcium solution is not promptly given by intravenous injection, death could result. Reoccurrence of the condition is rather common; therefore, the puppies should be permanently removed from the bitch and bottle fed as they may continue to deplete the bitch of calcium as they nurse.

MASTITIS

Bitches with more milk than they need can develop inflammation of the mammary glands, each of which ends in the teat from which the pups so hungrily draw their milk. Milk ac-

Some genetic research must be done to breed out undesirable traits in a breeding program. For instance, a breeder cannot use individual dogs that visibly carry unwanted traits if he does not want them to appear again. Mating tri-color dogs like this one will not produce bi-color puppies. Tri-color is pure recessive, and if two tri-colors are bred there will be no dominance for bi-color in the puppies.

The Wire Fox Terrier is one of the best known and most popular of the terriers. Of English origins, it is an ancient breed found in almost all English speaking countries.

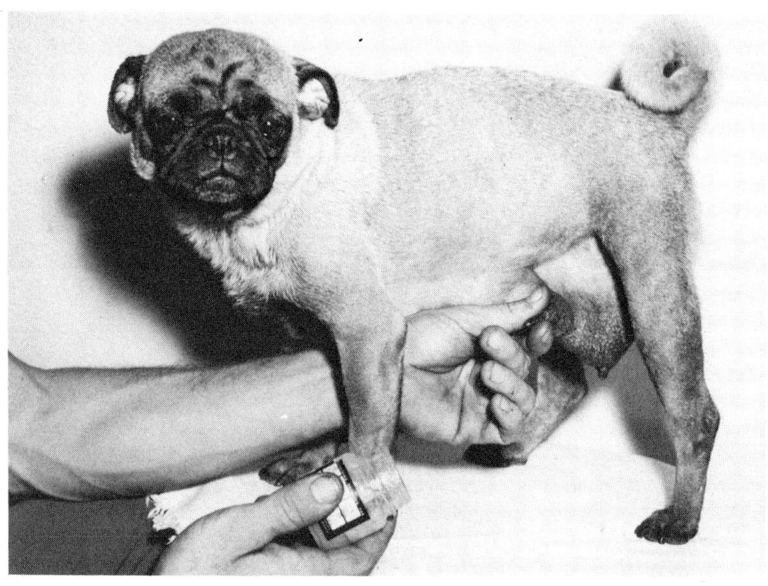

A dam may develop mastitis, a potentially painful condition involving inflammation of the mammary glands, where the teats become caked and engorged with unused milk. One treatment is to massage the affected area with petroleum jelly, then aspirate the milk away with a breast pump.

cumulates because (1) there may be too few pups to drink it, (2) pups suck from favorite teats, leaving some of them unused and gorged with milk or (3) some pups may be too sickly or weak to seek out, latch onto and suck enough from teats, which then may not be nursed. Also, (4) a teat may be too large, too small, too flat, or inverted. Bacterial contamination goes along with some of the above reasons for mastitis, and infections can complicate the engorged teat, making antibiotic treatment necessary.

If too much milk seems to be causing the problem, put a pup on a congested teat and perhaps it may draw off some of the extra milk before it becomes caked. Or, you can aspirate (with a breast pump) some of the milk away after massaging the teat with some olive oil. Preventive efforts are best, but medical measures may be required such as hormonal therapy and/or antibiotics in advanced cases. In extreme cases where the glands abcess, surgery may be indicated.

METRITIS

Extended whelping time or retained placentas can lead to inflammation and infection of the uterus (or metritis). The signs of disease include a swollen vulva, grayish-white pus discharge or bloody discharge with white flecks, fever, increased pulse rate (normal pulse ranges between ninety and one hundred beats per minute), loss of appetite, vomiting, and a characteristic pose: she crouches, somewhat upright, and rests on her elbows and hocks. Metritis may respond to antibiotics, but may progress to pyometra which almost invariably results in death if a hysterectomy is not done.

PROLAPSED UTERUS OR VAGINA

One horn or the body of the uterus may invert into the vagina and through the vulva, or the vagina itself may turn inside out.

After the first batch of births, this Labrador Retriever bitch rests awaiting the second.

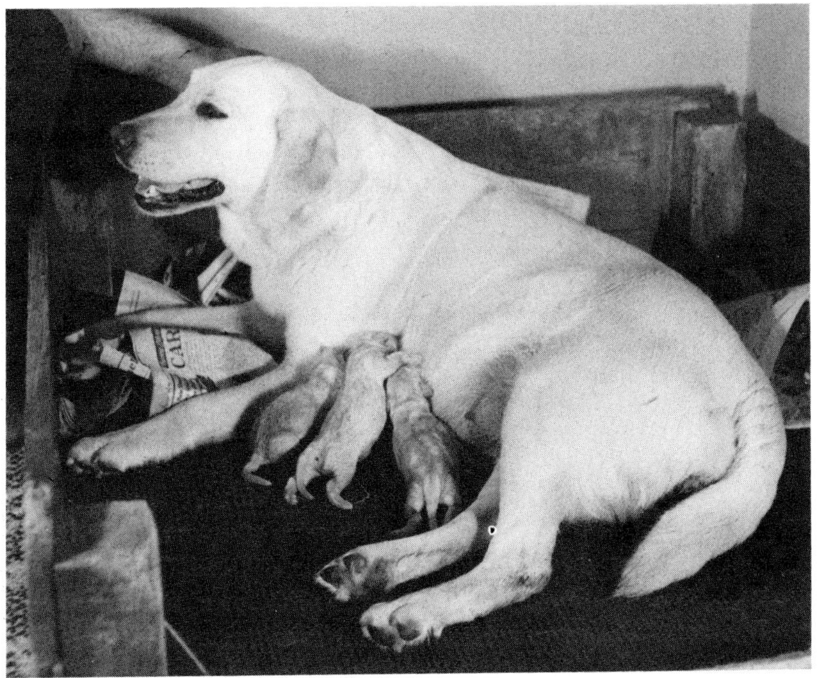

The earliest roots of this Shih Tzu puppy can be traced back to the forbidden city of Peking. Early breed standards for the Shih Tzu of the Peking Kennel Club as well as those of the United States and England, stated that all colors were permissible, but a white blaze on the head and tail tip were particularly desirable. In China where this little dog was a great favorite in the early history of the breed, the golden or honey color was most highly prized, and for a time western countries found it very difficult to obtain this color after the dog had been introduced to them.

The Siberian Husky, one of several northern breeds used primarily as sled dogs, is gentler and more civilized than its northern brothers. This is thought to be so because the Husky, unlike the others, was kept inside the shelter with its master, enjoying human companionship and learning to fit into the human scheme of things. The other breeds were staked outside in all types of weather and came into contact with humans only to be fed and worked by them.

If these Irish Setter pups follow the rapidly growing trend, they will not only be conspicuous in the conformational rings and obedience trials as adults, but will make their mark among the ranks of pointing dogs in field trials as well.

This is a surgical problem which may be corrected if prompt action is taken.

CAESAREAN SECTION

The operation of removing the pups by cutting into the abdomen and uterus of the bitch is generally safe; however, if the emergency Caesarean section follows a prolonged, exhausting and fruitless labor, the danger to the bitch is substantially increased.

Reasons for resorting to a Caesarean section include 1. dystocia due to an abnormally large pup, 2. one presenting in such a way that it cannot get out, is blocking the passage and birth of its littermates or is threatening the life of its dam, 3. an abnormal pelvis in the bitch which does not allow passage of the pups (such as a previous pelvic fracture), 4. inertia, 5. long and arduous labor which exhausts the bitch to the point where weakness causes the uterine and abdominal contractions to stop.

Your bitch can be operated on without losing consciousness if your veterinarian selects to operate with a hypnotic and local anesthesia. The local anesthetic is injected, the incision made, and the pups are taken from the semi-conscious bitch.

Gas anesthesia is the safest type of general anesthetic for delivering pups; if barbiturate anesthetics are used intravenously, the puppies may be quite effected by these drugs as they pass through the placental barrier.

Regardless of which method is used for the Caesarean section, the patient should be kept in a warm, clean bed after surgery until she recovers from the anesthesia. The pups should not be placed with the dam until she is once again alert. If the pups are also depressed from the anesthetic, artificial respiration may be required. It is imperative that the pups be kept dry and warm following the delivery.

Offer the puppies to their mother one at a time. After she licks a pup, help it to get settled on a teat and observe them carefully. Rarely, the bitch may not accept her puppies, but this may only be a temporary situation. Watch the mother when she goes out to do her duties; her sutures (stitches) should not be subjected to any undue strain. Short-legged breeds, such as the Dachshund, should not be permitted to climb stairs. Discourage the bitch from doing any excess walking, jumping or taking flying leaps back into the whelping box. Some mild exercise, of course, is desirable.

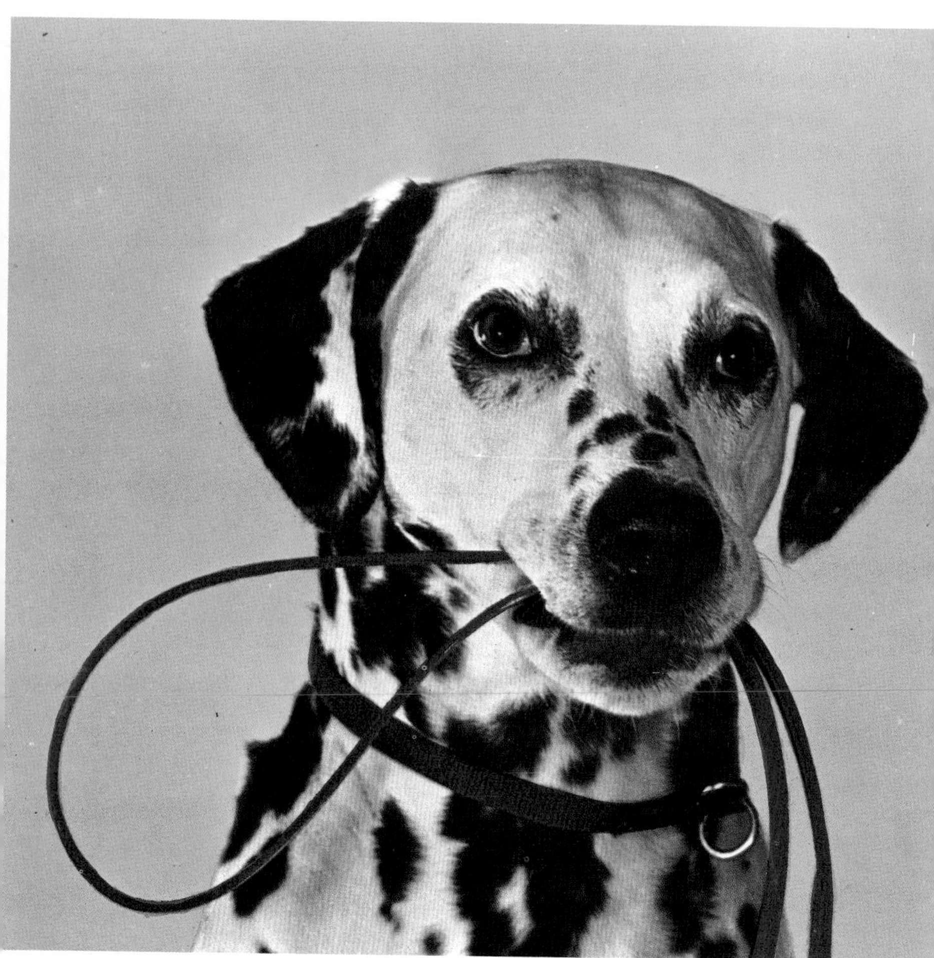

The Dalmatian has performed in just about every role assigned to a dog. But experts say his instinct for coaching horses is his strongest point. Not only has it been born in him, but bred and trained in him through the ages. Pictures of spotted dogs closely resembling the Dal in structure and type have been found.

One of the three most popular breeds of dogs in the United States, The German Shepherd has a calm temperament and strong sense of loyalty that makes him not just an ideal family pet, but also guardian of the family.

When puppies require supplemental feedings, they should be allowed to nurse at least the first 48 hours in order to get the vital colostral antibodies from their mother.

CHAPTER EIGHT

Puppyhood

FIRST DAYS OF THE PUP

As soon as it is determined to the best of your ability that the newborn puppy is essentially normal, keep it dry and make sure it gets a good meal. Most pups instinctively find a teat and start to nurse, but some may need assistance. Squeezing a drop of milk from the breast and placing his open mouth on the teat may be all the encouragement the slow puppy needs. Remember that colostrum which is very high in antibody content is very important to the newborn pup—don't be too hasty to get the pup onto a bitch milk substitute. Colostral antibodies are only available to the pup during the first 24 to 48 hours; after that the pup's digestive enzymes break down the antibodies. It is therefore highly desirable to let each pup nurse during the first day, even if this means alternating puppies in a very large litter that must be supplemented with bottle feeding.

If you do elect to destroy certain pups, for instance those with lethal defects, do it as humanely as possible, preferably taking them to a veterinarian.

In two or three days pups begin to crawl, pulling themselves along jerkily and wobbly, letting the head fall from side to side. They crawl in great circular routes and yelp until they touch something soft and warm. If this something is not the mother's teat, they nose around until they attach to one. Pups may utter vague little noises while feeding, sometimes because the milk is not coming fast enough. After sucking their fill, they perhaps doze off, hanging on a teat by suction after their meal. Healthy, adequately fed puppies sleep deeply and quietly between meals.

The Smooth Fox Terrier, one of two varieties of the Fox Terrier, is believed to have come from a different source than the Wire. Also of English origins, the Smooth is believed to have appeared in the show ring some 20 years after the wire.

Opposite:
Only in the United States is the Irish Setter self-colored in the rich mahogany coat for which he is so highly prized. His ancestors in Ireland, and many current relatives there and in other European countries even yet are red and white.

At ten to fourteen days of age, the puppies eyes will begin to open. Once the eye has begun to open it must not be allowed to become resealed with "sleep" as an infection may begin behind the eyelids. You can wipe this material off with a damp piece of cotton. Avoid bright light during this eye-opening process as excessive light may damage their vision.

WEANING

At two and one-half weeks, encourage the pup to try lapping up semi-solid food such as oatmeal with milk and some honey, or bottled baby food. Dip the tip of the pup's nose into a shallow plate of the food and when it instinctively licks off its nose, push its whole muzzle gently into the food. Pellets of finely chopped meat, or better yet, blended commercially available puppy food (made into a gruel with milk), can also be used to start the self-feeding. Too much semi-solid food and not enough nursing, however, can disrupt regular bowel movements.

At about three weeks of age the milk teeth begin to erupt. At this time be aware of the puppies' exaggerated sucking habits which are expressed by grabbing the closest suckable item (paws, ears, penises, etc.). If a puppy develops this habit, separate him from the other pups for awhile.

Weaning occurs about six to nine weeks after whelping, and can be a shock to problem puppies. During the transition period from teat sucking to self-feeding, the pup can certainly be allowed to share the mother's food, but only if she permits it. Do not rush or force the weaning process if it is not necessary as this leads to digestive upsets in the puppies and caked breasts in the bitch. If the bitch's breasts seem distended or hard (overly full), it means the bitch should be nursed more heavily by the puppies. Nature's way of weaning the puppies is a gradual process. At this period of puppy development the bitch will spend less and less time nursing the puppies and thereby force their growing appetites to be satisfied from other sources. A reduced production of milk will gradually occur with decreased demand by the puppies. This reduction can be further encouraged by reducing the caloric intake of the bitch (i.e. reducing the quantity of food).

It is advisable to let pups try only one new food at a time, giving

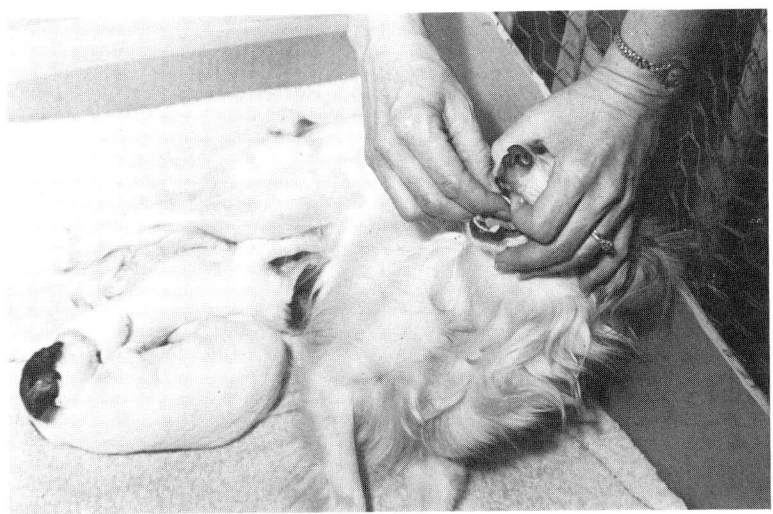

While she is nursing, the bitch needs about three times more food than during the first few weeks of pregnancy. Dietary supplements are available either in tablet form or as food additives. They should be used in balance; too much of one can cause a deficiency of another.

In between the four or six times a day puppies usually eat, it may be advantageous to give a snack. This pup, like most being weaned, seems to think getting into the bowl makes eating easier.

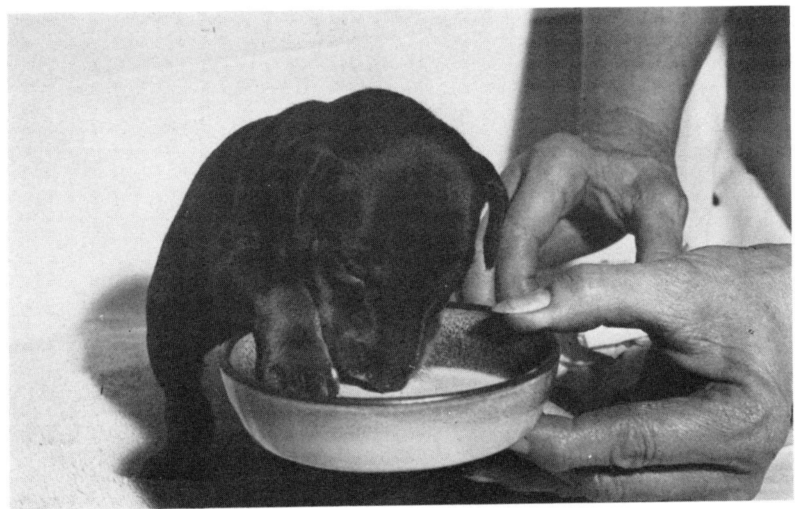

His rich, luxurious coat is the most striking thing about the rough-coated Collie. It was probably developed under the same rugged outdoor conditions that promoted thick wool on the sheep his breed have for centuries watched over and herded.

Fashionable pet of Victorian aristocrats, the Yorkshire Terrier's extremely long and hard-to-care-for coat almost demanded that it be kept indoors where it would not get matted and tangled. A modern breed created and developed around Lancashire and Yorkshire, England, the Yorkie's history falls with the range of organized dogdom.

it once, then twice daily until the weaning is over. The process generally takes from five to six weeks to completely wean the puppies.

By eight weeks the pup will generally urinate and have its bowel movements in the same place each time—hopefully this will be a spot far from its food saucer. From eight to twelve weeks the pup urinates every two hours; excitement decreases the interval. After twelve weeks, the pup goes for longer periods without urinating. As a general rule, however, the pups will also have to urinate upon waking up.

Bitches keep their pups clean if their whelping box is small enough to encourage the pups (when old enough) to climb out of the box to do their duties. The bitch's alacrity in keeping her box clean usually lasts as long as the pups are not eating the same food that she does. Pay constant attention to the bitch's health. Your veterinarian can tell you just what mineral and vitamin supplements she may need to help her through the weaning, as well as during pregnancy and lactation.

A private feeding saucer is a device that is commonly used to help out with the over-hungry pup. Problem eaters, on the other

The weaning process should begin when the puppies are about two and a half weeks old. They can be started on a gruel mixture of oatmeal and milk, adding more solids as they get their teeth.

These eager pups look as if they are about to burst out of their pen, led by the one standing at the door. By the time puppies are four to five weeks old, a pack leader has usually emerged.

hand, may be stimulated to eat by putting their food out of their saucers on the floor or at the bottom of the whelping box.

By five to six weeks you have gradually stepped up the pup's diet to four meals daily of a nutritionally balanced diet. At eight to twelve weeks, you are feeding them every six to eight hours daily. Offering dry food in a bowl (free choice) will satisfy those slow eaters in the litter. Do not, however, allow pups to overeat to the point where they become overweight butterballs. Obesity is not healthy in puppies nor older dogs.

Here are some additional notes on weaning diets that have been found to be useful by breeders and veterinarians. Be aware that any guidelines to feeding are, of course, dependent on your own particular dog and your own unique dog housing situation. Puppies can eat four to six times a day, the exact number of the meals and when to change the quantity depends on the breed and with the age as well as with individual idiosyncracies. Five- or six-week-old pups generally get four meals daily, dropping down to about two meals when their age reaches three to six months. Just watch the pup and his eating pace. When he consistently looses interest in a meal, drop it from the feeding schedule. Finally, sometime between six months and one year after whelping, one meal a day may be sufficient. The following chart will give some idea of how much food is required for a dog according to its weight:

Hailing originally from Scotland, the West Highland White Terrier traces its roots to the Malcolm family of Poltallock. Reputedly a reddish or buff color in its early days, the White strain of Westie was said to be developed by Colonel Malcolm, who used the Westie as a hunting dog, to distinguish him readily from the game being hunted.

Opposite:
Originally bred to be a gun dog, the hunting instincts of the red Irish Setter have taken second place in breeding programs to his lovely rich mahogany coat and spirited, gay personality that make him a stand-out in conformational show rings.

Food Needed According To Dog Weight

		Dog Weight (lbs.)							
		5	10	15	20	30	50	70	110
Dry Meal	Adult Food (lbs.)	0.2	0.34	0.42	0.54	0.78	1.25	1.75	2.75
	Puppy Food (lbs.)	0.4	0.68	0.84	1.08	1.56	.50	3.50	*
Moist (Canned) Food	Adult Food (lbs.)	0.55	0.93	1.18	1.52	2.14	3.44	4.83	7.60
	Puppy Food (lbs.)	1.1	1.86	2.34	3.04	4.26	6.90	9.86	*

* These "puppies" are so big that the owner has to use common sense.

Although varying charts can be made as to the caloric requirements of dogs, remember that they are all individuals, each with their own basic metabolic rates and degrees of activity. Littermates may vary three-fold in their individual caloric requirements.

At twenty days, the upper canines may start to show. At three weeks, the pup may drink from a saucer or even eat semi-solids, including the predigested food some bitches regurgitate for their pups. Also at three weeks, the pup growls, paws the ground, stands up, and halfway crawls and walks in all directions, describing dizzy circles, urinating and moving its bowels from time to time without being stimulated by their mother's licking.

Normal, healthy progress in a pup means regular and progressive weight gain. Use scales if you want to keep precise records. A pup who gains, eats heartily, sleeps soundly and moves vigorously is healthy.

BEHAVIOR

After the first three weeks your pup begins to recognize its littermates and you. A pack leader usually emerges towards the fourth or fifth week, and the whole litter is let out in a mob rush to say

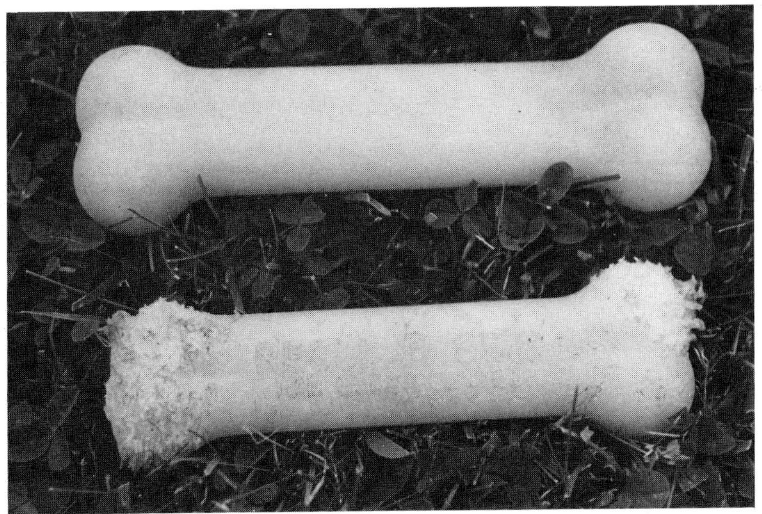

Nylabone, a ham-flavored nylon chew toy, is a safe and beneficial way for both puppies and adult dogs to exercise teeth and massage gums. Unlike many other such doggie toys on the market today, Nylabone will not chip and break causing possible injury or even death from splintered pieces getting caught in the dog's throat or stomach. As dogs chew on it the nylon bone frills, becoming a doggie toothbrush.

"good morning" to owner and visitors. But do not confuse puppy rough-housing with serious fights. A rough-and-tumble stage is to be expected of healthy pups. Several pups may be lodged together in separate little kennels if fighting becomes a serious problem as they get older. Return any pups from this "solitary confinement" with care. Littermates may rush and seriously injure the returned ones.

Rough play in pups should not be entirely discouraged, at least when the size of the pup is not beyond certain limits. If jumping becomes a menace from a larger pup, try to discourage it by firmly but not too painfully squeezing its paws while instructing it to get "down!".

Doggie toys can be improvised quite inexpensively, or they can be selected from a long line of such products at any well-stocked pet shop. Commercially prepared bones without any sharp edges, such as Nylabone®, make good chewables. Rubber balls are good

This long-haired Dachshund puppy is one of three varieties of the breed that has enjoyed the popularity of the ten most favored breeds in European countries. While the smooth haired variety is the best known, demand for the elegant long-haired is rapidly growing.

Opposite:
The Maremma Sheepdog is little known outside of his native Italy, but there he has been used for centuries to help shepherds with their flocks. Related to the Great Pyrenees and the Hungarian Kuvasz, the coat of the Maremma is usually pure white, sometimes with fawn markings, and kept meticulously clean.

if they are large enough not to be swallowed and cannot be chewed into small portions. Fragments of toys can be swallowed and cause serious gastrointestinal problems, such as an intestinal blockage.

Up to sixteen weeks, pups really do not need any organized exercise or walks, but you should begin simple behavior training as soon as possible. Do not encourage any behavior which you would not want continued.

DENTAL CONSIDERATIONS

Teeth first appear in about three to five weeks. These widely spaced, brittle "milk teeth" are softer and sharper than the pup's permanent teeth will be. Permanent teeth gradually push their way through the gums after the milk teeth roots have been absorbed and the deciduous teeth loosen and are shed.

The permanent teeth of most breeds are supposed to be arranged in what is called a scissor bite—teeth meet in front, the tips of the uppers overlapping the tips of the lowers. An undershot mouth, however, is the breed standard for some dogs—the lower jaw and lower teeth extend beyond the upper front teeth. An overshot mouth has the upper front teeth extending out over the lowers—a fault, not a desired breed standard. Another fault is for upper front and lower front teeth to meet edge on edge, that is, with no overlapping.

A lot of mouth activity—chewing, biting, sucking—characterize the newly found teeth, but puppy gums can be quite sensitive at this stage.

At about twelve to sixteen weeks, permanent teeth begin to appear. Dogs generally have forty-two permanent teeth; however, dolichocephalic breeds (long muzzled) have forty-four and brachycephalic (short muzzled) breeds have fewer than normal. Availability of chewable items is helpful in aiding the pup to get rid of all the deciduous teeth at the proper times. Due to abnormal or complete lack of root resorption, retention of deciduous teeth is the most common dental problem in puppies. Retention of these deciduous teeth can lead to abnormal positioning of the permanent teeth. To avoid this, extraction of the retained puppy teeth may occasionally be necessary.

Another way to encourage loose milk teeth to come out is to let the pup play with a strip of burlap or other loosely woven

In most breeds, an undershot jaw is a defect caused by too closely inbreeding relatives. The Bulldog, however, is one of the few in which the considerably undershot lower jaw is a conformational requirement.

The Pembroke Welsh Corgi bears a striking resemblance to the Cardigan Welsh Corgi, and both were used for the same purpose—as cattle dogs. Though the Pembroke is supposed to be a younger breed, still his progenitors go back to 1100. The most readily noticeable difference between the two breeds are the tail, the Pembroke's is docked as short as possible while the Cardigan's is long, and the ears, the Pembroke's are pointed and the Cardigan's rounded.

The coat of this Yorkshire Terrier puppy is a distinct black and tan in color. As an adult he will be a dark steel blue and tan, the tan being darker at the roots than in the middle, and even lighter at the tips.

material. By snagging the loose tooth on a loop in the fabric, a slight tug may be sufficient to remove the problem tooth.

The first visible permanent teeth appear at approximately sixteen weeks of age. Initially the two upper mid-incisors appear, followed by the upper molars. At approximately six months of age the pup should have its permanent teeth.

Previous illnesses in which fever was prominent can cause the permanent teeth to appear mottled. A feverish condition is not the only thing that can damage the cells responsible for enamel production. Tetracycline, a broad spectrum antibiotic, can stain the permanent teeth if administered during the development of these teeth. To avoid this permanent yellowing condition, never use Tetracycline during the first few months of the pup's life.

USE AND ABUSE OF TEETH

Incisors cut, gnaw and comb out the coat. Canines grip, carry and tear. Pre-molars and molars cut. Upper and lower pre-molars work together (that is, work together against one another!) to break up the size of food. Dogs do little or no chewing—with pre-

Playing with a piece of burlap or a loosely woven blanket is a good way for puppies to dispose of deciduous milk teeth. The open weave snags the loose teeth, easily removing them to make way for permanent teeth.

Because of their short muzzle, Pugs and other brachycephalic breeds frequently have fewer than the normal number of 42 permanent teeth.

sent day dog foods, in fact, dogs can do quite well without teeth should they loose all of them with old age.

Dogs are subject to tartar accumulation on the teeth, as are humans. Teeth may normally acquire a coat of yellowish tartar which collects bacteria, causes bad breath and even pushes back the gumline, thereby exposing the roots of the teeth to infection, abcessation and perhaps loss. Dry foods and biscuit bones minimize tartar accumulation, but some dogs may require mechanical removal of this tartar if excessive accumulation occurs. Bad teeth and the resulting dental infection can cause serious health problems. For example, if the invading bacteria become distributed throughout the circulatory system, endocarditis with its resultant heart valve damage may occur.

This Welsh Corgi puppy, small enough to fit into a wicker Cornucopia now, at maturity will weigh approximately 26 pounds. Though he is short-legged and travels very close to the ground, the breed was used principally as a cattledog, driving cattle by nipping at their heels. His intelligence and one-time use as a guardian of children stand him in good stead as an ideal family pet.

In most breeds, permanent teeth, appearing between three and four months of age, number 42. Long-muzzled (dolichocephalic) breeds like the Borzoi have 44.

NAILS AND DEWCLAWS

The sharp nails of nursing pups can dig painfully into the mother, so much so that she may even stop feeding them. Pups' nails should be cut (without getting to the "quick" or tissue) once weekly until they are four weeks old, then at greater intervals as required by the various dogs.

The functionless dewclaws may be removed when puppies are one to four days old, but be sure to check established breed standards and requirements. With St. Bernards, dewclaws are optional, and with German Shepherds, the front dewclaws should never be removed although the rear ones can be clipped off, if they are present. If one leaves them on and forgets to trim them, they will grow around in a circle, perhaps penetrating into the toe pad. Dewclaws can hook on objects which can tear them off—quite a painful accident—and start a hemorrhage. Although some owners snip the dewclaws off with scissors (boiled for at least 20 minutes) and then put some antiseptic and astringent powder on the wound, the veterinarian can do it quickly, safely and in such a way as to avoid unsightly scarring.

EYE CARE

Eyes open for the first time anytime from day 7 to 13. It is abnormal for pups just born to have opened eyes. Delayed opening, if due to stickiness, can be remedied by wiping (perhaps with ophthalmic yellow oxide of mercury ointment or other ointments recommended by your veterinarian) from the inside to the outside corner of the eye, cleaning away any crusty substance. Avoid strong light, especially from lights meant to heat the whelps, until the pups' eyes have been opened for several weeks. If the lids appear swollen or puffy, it could be due to a bacterial infection, which, if left untreated, could lead to permanent corneal damage and blindness. Treatment consists of opening the lids to allow drainage of pus and application of ophthalmic antibiotic preparations. Clouding over of the eye can be caused by infection or may follow scratches by nails from playful littermates.

CLEFT PALATE AND HAIRLIP

Short muzzled (brachycephalic) breeds seem to have more problems with a split upper lip (hairlip) and cleft palates than other breeds. Nursing is encumbered because sucking is not adequate to pull in milk and what does come in goes up through the palate defect and into the nasal passages. Mild cases may survive, but puppies with serious cleft palates are either put to sleep or the defect must be surgically repaired.

The herding and guarding instincts of the Great Pyrenees mountain dog carries over naturally to the children of the family. Possessed of a serenity and majesty, the Pyr is sensitive to the moods of his human companions. He makes an ideal pet in another respect, and that is in spite of his large size, 100 to 125 pounds at maturity, his calm temperament and low metabolism keep his food requirements less than smaller dogs of a more active and high strung nature.

Like many breeds, the origins of the St. Bernard are obscure, but legends of their missions of mercy seem to be well-founded. The rescue work these dogs performed at the Great St. Bernard pass in the Swiss Alps was recorded in the early 1700's with the implication that it had been taken for granted there a long time. Besides their excellent pathfinding abilities and keen sense of smell, the dogs are said to possess an uncanny capacity to sense the onset of an avalanche.

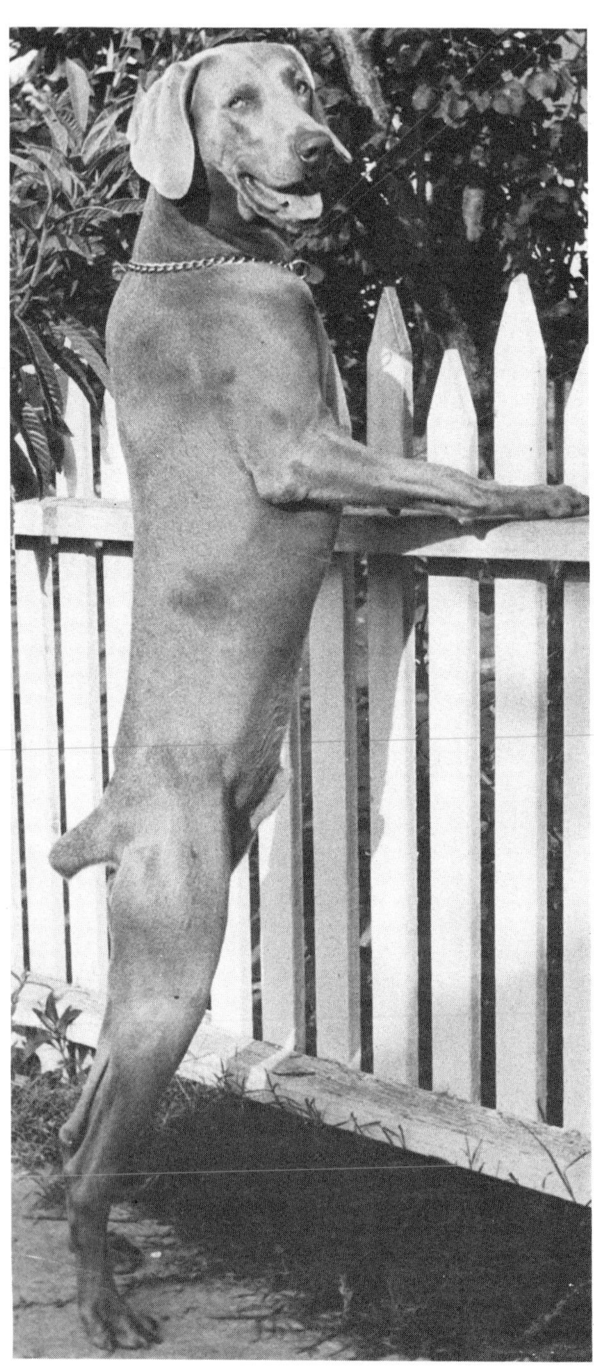

Tail docking is usually done when the pup is two or three days old. According to the breed, tail lengths vary from practically nothing at all, as in the Old English Sheepdog, to the Weimaraner's tail, which must be six inches long at maturity to satisfy the standard.

EARS

A pup's ears begin to open around the tenth day after birth. The external ear canal must be kept clean and free of excessive accumulations of wax. Long-haired breeds are prone to accumulate lots of hair in the outer ear and this hinders air circulation and may predispose the dog to acquiring an ear infection. Dog groomers and veterinarians alike cannot seem to reach a consensus of opinion as to whether this excessive hair should be plucked from the ear canal or left alone. Whatever works best for the particular dog in question is probably the best policy.

DOCKING OF TAIL

Puppies of some breeds are born with bobbed tails, but most pups need a special docking operation if they are to have such tails. Docking can be done on the day the dewclaws are cut, although some breeders wait as late as the fifth day. If too little of

In certain breeds such as the Great Pyrenees the presence of dewclaws, a recessive condition, is necessary for conformity to the standard. In certain other breeds dewclaws are a defect.

This Boxer pup
sports a white
mask instead
the more usua
black one com
mon to the
breed. White
color in the
Boxer bespeak
its relationship
to many other
bulldog types,
but according
the standard
white must be
restricted to
one third of th
ground color.

The comically doleful look of the Basset Hound gives him an instant appeal. This dog that's been described as half a dog high and two dogs long seems aware that he will never win a beauty contest and makes up with his clownish loving disposition for what he lacks in looks.

the tail is cut off, a clever trimming can make a tail seem shorter, or can be done again later when the pup is older. The author remembers hearing tell of an itinerant black man who earned his living by biting off puppy tails for 5¢ a piece. Better let your veterinarian do it for you, unless you have become proficient at cutting off tails aseptically and accurately without excessive bleeding. If you've ever seen a dog running around with an ugly stump for a tail—only a scar and no hair on the distal tip—it was probably caused by someone untrained in docking tails who was out to save a few dollars. Not only can untrained persons cause a permanent flaw, but also their lack of antiseptic techniques could lead to an infection. Removing the distal portion of the tail by using rubber band compression is strongly discouraged. Although a tight ligature will result in the death and sloughage of the distal portion of the tail, it could also lead to a tetanus infection.

Special attention to eyes must be given hounds that actively pursue the chase. Because their quarry frequently leads them full tilt through densely brushy areas, their eyes are susceptible to infection caused by dirt, sand, pieces of bark, pollen, chemicals and other foreign matter.

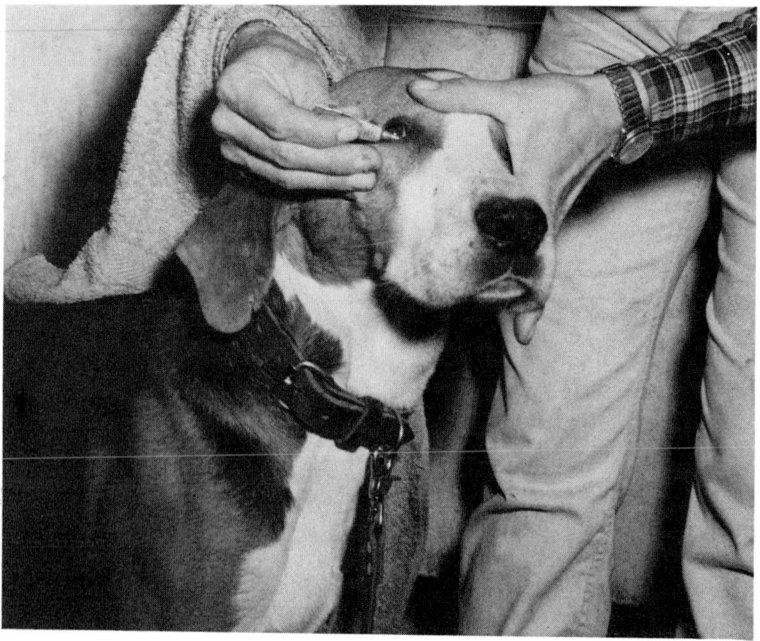

Puppies' eyes will remain closed until the pups are about ten days old. When they begin to open, keep them from resealing with sleep by wiping with damp cotton.

CROPPING THE EARS

"Redesigning" or cropping ears involves cutting the outer edge of the ear, (hopefully) making it stand erect and to a point. This surgical procedure is generally done at about eight to twelve weeks of age. Although cropping is frowned upon by many dog owners and breeders (indeed, it is even prohibited in England), it is still commonly done in some breeds.

Originally, fighting dogs had ears cropped to protect them from being torn by the other dogs, or whatever animals upon which the fighting dogs were set. Tail docking is done by some owners right

Dalmatian puppies are born pure white. Their unique spotting which develops with age, is a culmination of centuries of selective breeding.

Opposite:

A prospective pet owner should not mistrust his inclination to reach out and grab this furry little ball of white fluff as his final choice. The hardiness of the West Highland White Terrier makes him an ideal family companion who loves to romp outdoors in frozen weather. As show dogs, they are a joy because they require very little trimming to keep them up to par.

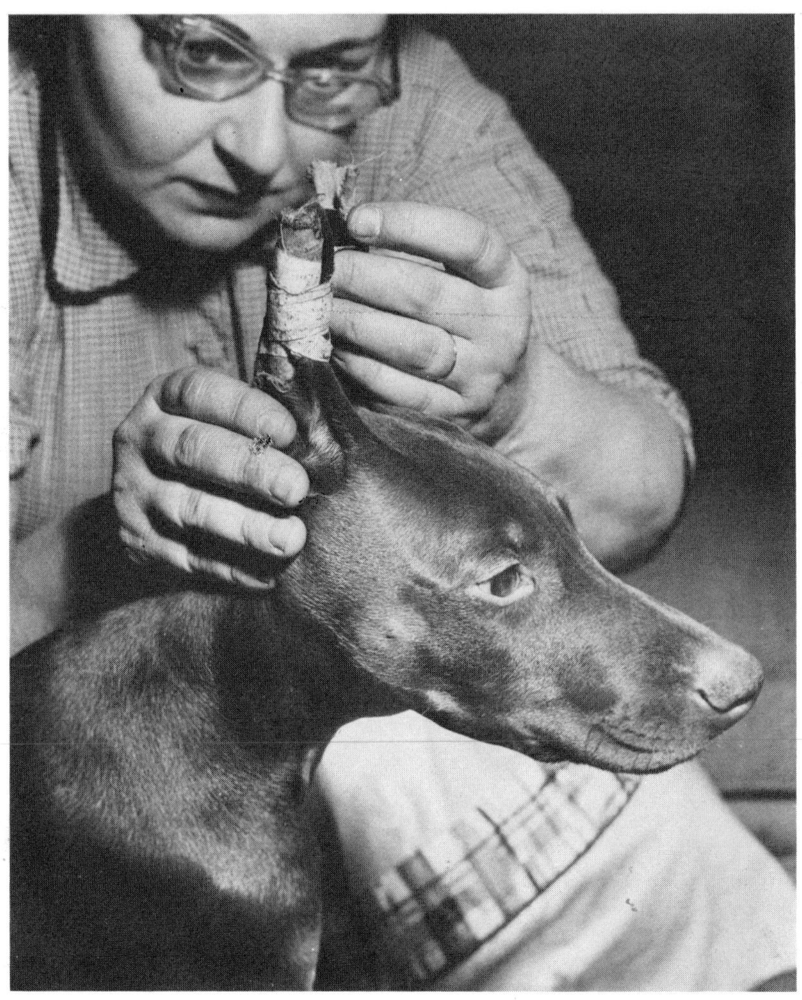

The Doberman Pinscher (above) and the Great Dane (opposite) are among a few breeds in the United States that regularly have their ears cropped. The hoped-for result is that the ears will stand erect and come to a point. It is a surgical procedure that should be done only by a veterinarian.

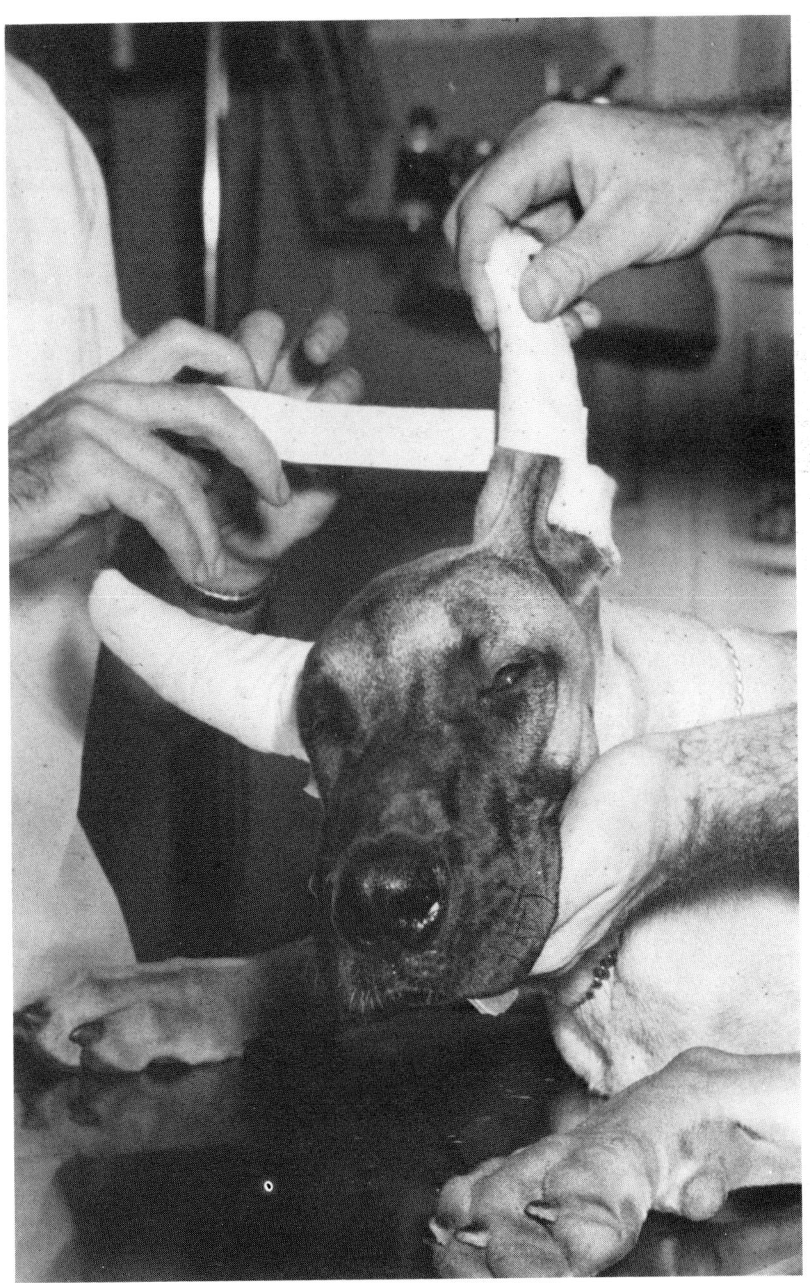

At first glance there seems to be very little difference among the many springers and cocker spaniels recognized by the American Kennel Club. But the Welsh Springer Spaniel shown distinguishes himself from his English and American Cocker and Springer relatives by the exclusivity of his red and white coat. No other color is acceptable according to the standard for the breed.

Oppostite:
English Cocker Spaniels, like this one, closely resembling their American cousins, were interbred with the American type for years. And American Cockers were frequently entered in the show ring as English on the basis of their larger size, which was one of the only characteristics dividing the two strains.

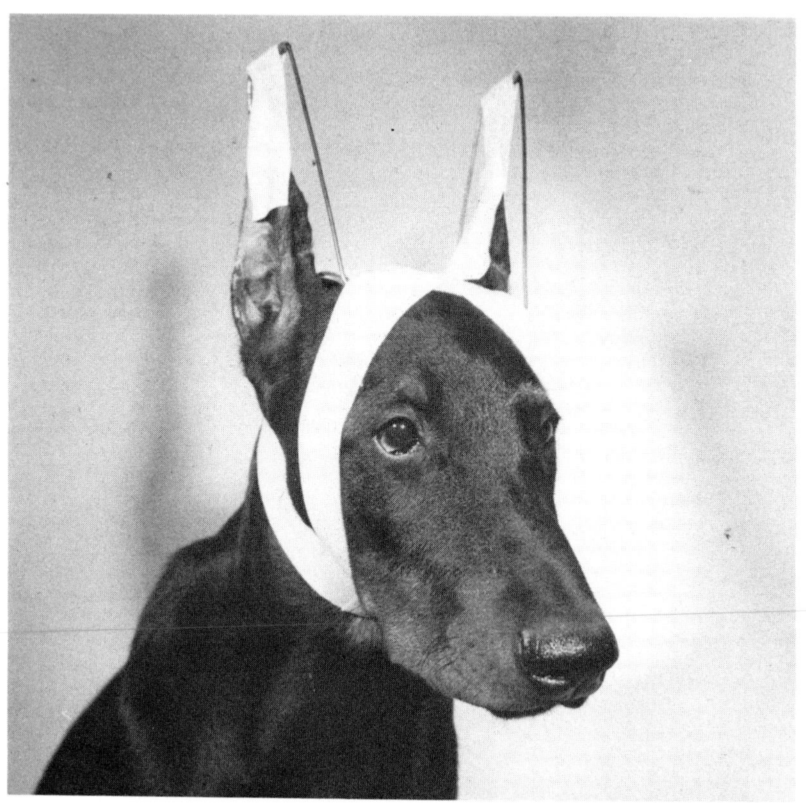

Dobe pup in an ear rack during final stages of ear-cropping. Ears are usually cropped between two and three months of age.

Opposite:
This four-month-old Great Dane pup demonstrates the results of a successful ear cropping operation.

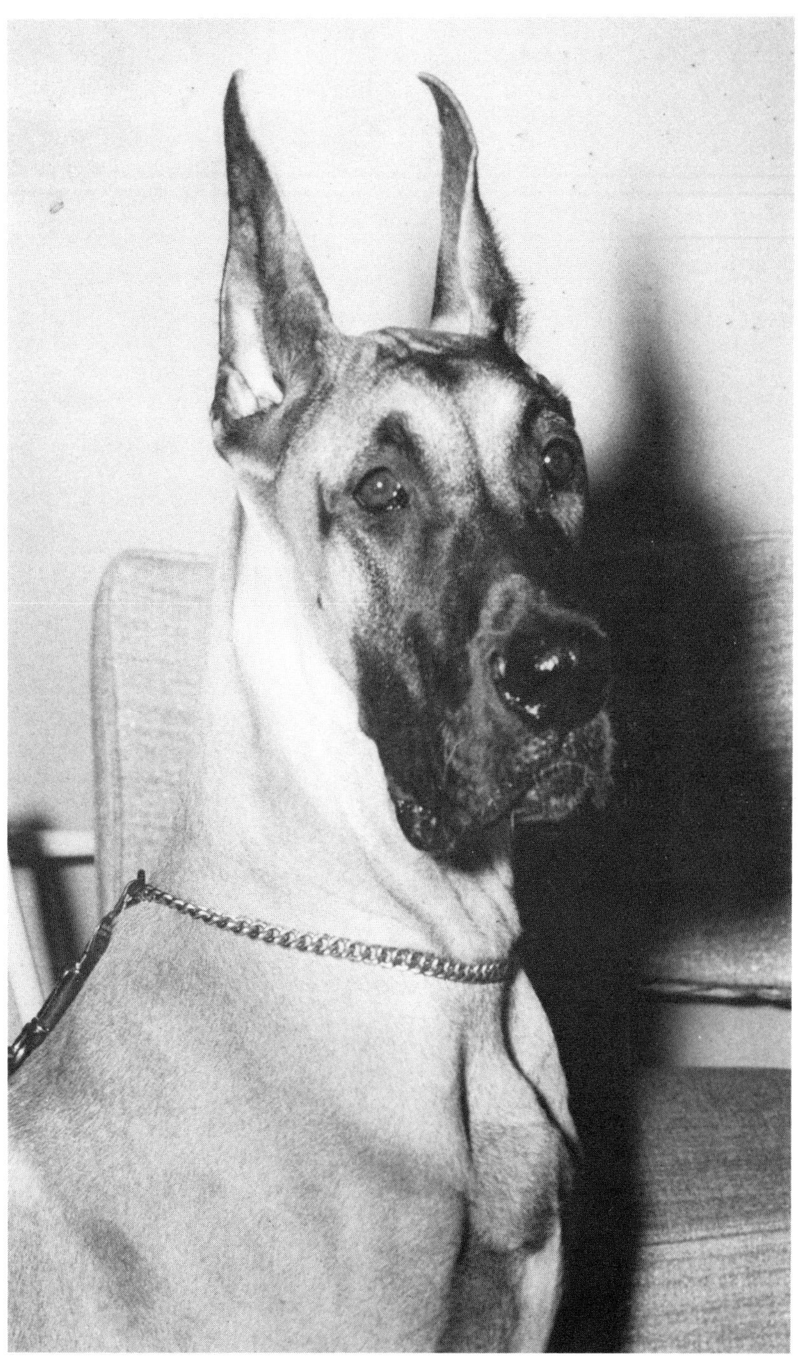

The Poodle may be the only breed of dog for which more than 150 ways exist to style his dense coat. In Germany and France where it gained fame as a water retriever, it was a practice to shear away parts of the coat to facilitate his water activities. It is believed that the custom of clipping the Poodle's hair in so many different styles began with this retriever clip.

These Bloodhound puppies, if well bred, will share the renown of their breed's ability to pick up and follow a trail. So accurate is the Bloodhound's instinct that his findings have been admitted as evidence in courts of law.

in the kennel, but cropping of ears is strictly a surgical matter and should only be performed under general anesthesia by veterinarians.

PARASITES

When pups are four to six weeks old, have stool specimens examined for worm eggs and other intestinal parasites. Proper identification of the parasites is required in order that the appropriate anthelmintic (dewormer) can be selected. Dosage is also critical as an overdose can cause serious problems or even death. Not all puppies have intestinal parasites and quite naturally, no treatment is necessary if parasites are not present. Because dogs can readily become infected and reinfected with intestinal parasites, stool specimens should be examined on a routine basis.

Although most parasites are host specific (a dog in this case) and do not readily infect other species, some overlapping of species susceptibility does exist. This is especially true of the developing larval stages of the adult parasite. Larvae oftentimes infect a wide variety of animals, man included.

Some of the physical signs of disease which suggest intestinal parasitism include a distended abdomen, prominent ribs, the spine showing through a dull coat, bloodless or anemic-looking gums and diarrhea. Scooting, (also called sledding, or sleigh-riding) along the floor while in a sitting position is indicative of anal itching. This is most probably due to overfilled anal glands and not to intestinal parasites; however, tapeworm proglottides which may crawl around the anal orifice can also cause the dog to scoot.

Roundworms appear as whitish or dirty pink, glistening watch springs or spaghetti-like lengths one and one-half to seven inches long. Hookworms are hair-thin and attain lengths of three-eighths to three fourths-inch. Whipworms taper in thickness (like a whip thickening in girth as it approaches the whip handle) from hair-thickness to double that. Tapeworms are flat, like a tape measure, or like translucent pieces of ribbon, and range in size from one-eighth inch to sixteen feet. The smaller fragments look like rice, and may be mixed up in the feces. Seldom are these adult worms seen, but must be detected by microscopic examination of stool specimens and identification of their characteristic eggs.

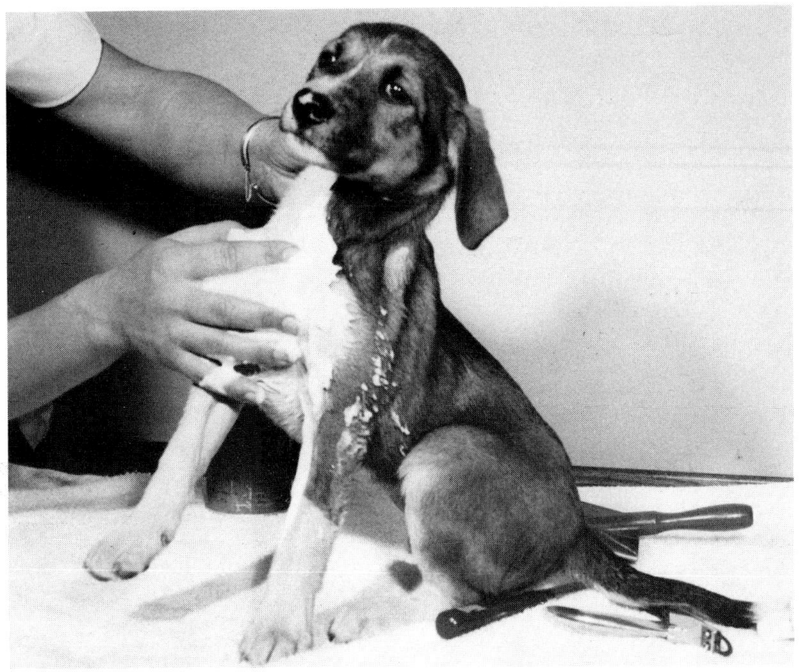

A dry bath, shampoo in a pressurized can available at most pet stores, is one way to rid puppies of external parasites that are often carriers of more harmful internal disease carriers without the risk of his catching a cold.

Fleas may carry tapeworm larvae, as well as cause itching, dermatitis and perhaps even anemia when the infestation is heavy. Control of these pests can be accomplished by using a name-brand spray or powder available at reliable pet shops. Follow the manufacturer's directions closely—these chemicals are toxic or they would not be effective.

Ticks can carry human as well as dog diseases. They also can cause an unpleasant skin irritation. When the dog bites and gnaws at the irritated area, dermatitis results. Flea and tick collars are of variable effectiveness depending upon the active ingredients, age of the collar, storage conditions, etc. Because most of these collars volitilize the active ingredient, once the toxic vapor is gone the collar is no longer effective. Ticks are relatively resistant to the ef-

Developed to scent a trail and follow it underground or into a den, the Dachshund's structure is peculiarly fitted to his purpose. Ideally his back should be of medium length for work below and close above the ground. Too short a back lacks the flexibilty for bends in underground dens; one that is too long is not well supported by the legs, and the dog tires easily.

These Blenheims are one of the varieties of English Toy Spaniel which while developed chiefly in England are believed to have their very earliest beginnings in Japan or China. Far eastern breeding is thought to account for the very short nose and other dwarfed features of the breed.

fects of insecticides as compared to fleas and lice. Always follow the manufacturers' recommendations to assure both safety and effectiveness of the collar. Also do not allow flea collars to get wet, as it may cause considerable irritation to the skin.

Lice are rarely found on dogs unless they are living in an unsanitary environment or are suffering from malnutrition or general debilitation.

Skin mites are minute parasites that live in the hair follicles (Demodex) or burrow in tunnels through the various skin layers. The type of dermatitis they cause is commonly called mange. If you think your dog is infected with mange mites, consult your veterinarian for an accurate diagnosis and appropriate medication. The lesions can advance rather rapidly and if not properly treated may lead to very severe complications.

PROTRUDING NAVEL

Congenital umbilical hernia occurs more often in some breeds than others. There is some evidence of an inherited weakness of

Mange must be treated promptly, since the lesions that accompany it rapidly progress. Mange is caused by minute skin parasites that live in the hair follicles or tunnel through the various layers of skin.

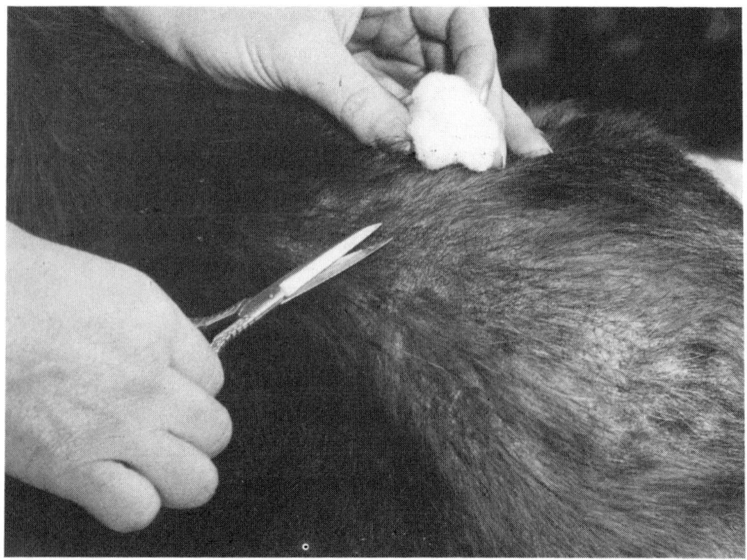

the tissues which may predispose animals to acquiring hernias in several areas. Although some umbilical hernias are unavoidable, they are less apt to occur if you refrain from pulling on the umbilical cord when the pup is born. Surgical repair of umbilical hernias is not always necessary; trust your veterinarian's judgment based upon the size and severity of the defect.

DIARRHEA

Diarrhea may only be transient and, in time, clear up, however, it should always be considered serious and the cause found and corrected. Puppies are very prone to dehydration due to excessive fluid loss in the stools. If these pups are not promptly rehydrated, death can result. Blood or mucus in the stools indicates the diarrhea is particularly bad. This condition should be brought to the veterinarian's attention at once.

Diarrhea is most often caused by one or more of the following conditions: (1) dietary upset from an inappropriate diet; (2) ingestion of foreign material such as leaves, grass, bones or fragments of toys; (3) intestinal parasites; or (4) bacterial or viral pathogens which have invaded the intestinal walls.

When diarrhea occurs, clean up the area to avoid further contamination and isolate the pup in case the cause of the diarrhea is infectious. Withhold food and milk but allow the pup to drink water at frequent intervals. The pup should then be placed on a very bland, easily digested diet such as cottage cheese, boiled rice and cooked eggs. In severe cases of diarrhea the rectum may prolapse. If this occurs, try gently pushing it in using a cold moistened cotton wad and consult your veterinarian should the problem reoccur.

REVIVING A PUP

When an apparently lifeless pup is noticed, try to revive it by placing it on or in a warm area (avoid using electric heating pads—hot water bottles are much safer). Massage the pup vigorously and give artificial respiration if it has stopped breathing. This is done by repeatedly impressing and releasing the rib cage. A dog on his way to recovery generally moves in response to physical stimuli.

Pet shops carry a wide range of carrying cases for transporting the bitch to the mating place or a puppy to a new home. The one shown is designed to be used three different ways. As a carrying case it is equipped with a "bumper" around the outside of the case to prevent other packages or luggage from being packed tightly against it and cutting off air to the animal inside. It can also be taken apart to serve as a bed or an indoor retreat the dog can enter or leave at will.

PUPPY HOUSING

Whatever is chosen for bedding, watch out for holes and tears, especially in blankets with loose strands which can twist around tiny necks. Ideal bedding, in general, should not present any danger to animals; it should not stain, be toxic or be edible, and it must be free of disease-causing organisms or dust. In addition, the material should be dry, absorb moisture, be disposable, be easily obtainable and easy to store, and be economical enough for the quantities you may need to have of it. Change the bedding frequently, using only clean, dry material.

The littermates who do not quarrel may sleep together in one bed, placed in a draft-free area. Set newspapers outside the bedding box and the pups will soon learn to use them for their duties. Instinctively, a pup crawls away from his bed to urinate out of the box providing that the box is small enough (otherwise, the pup thinks a far corner of a spacious box is far enough away from its bed).

If you have several litters of puppies at a time, the effort expended on a puppy house with a thermostat, fencing and runs will be quite a worthwhile investment. Do not build puppy runs in line with the prevailing wind unless you build up the side, too. A canopy or other (non-heat intensifying) roofing is a good idea for either hot or rainy climates. A canopy also protects pups from "Sir Isaac Newton Disease". . . falling coconuts or even apples can injure or even kill adult dogs, let alone pups.

CATCHING AND PICKING UP A PUP

Once the pup starts meandering about, do not scare it by trying to hook it with a hockey stick whenever it hides under the sofa. Coaxing, perhaps with some choice tidbit, may work just as well. If it still does not show, ignore it. Pups are curious creatures and will probably soon come out to see what you are doing now that you are not chasing them!

Strong, squirming pups, when lifted, must be held firmly but without painfully squeezing them. Take them up by both shoulders and place one arm or hand under their hindquarters for support. Pick up larger dogs by making like a forklift with your arms, one under the chest and one further down, or behind the thighs or hind legs. Handling a dog should be often enough for taming, but not enough for spoiling. Handling your dog really begins with the first pat on its tiny head. Brushing and grooming go hand in hand with handling and training for the dog must let itself be groomed; show dogs, especially, must allow themselves to be handled enough to be placed in show position. Some breeds are more hairy than others and need frequent grooming, especially long-haired shedders when they are shedding their baby coat. Note, however, that some breeds (Maltese, poodles) do not shed puppy coats.

If a long-haired pup gets too dirty, it may need to be washed in a warm environment with a mild soap or shampoo. Keep the puppy warm until thoroughly dry. Some dog owners have a tendency to bathe their dogs too often; this can result in dry skin, itching and

To pick up a strong, squirming puppy, use one arm to support its chest close to the front legs and the other arm to give support closer to the abdomen.

dermatitis. In most cases, six to eight baths per year should be sufficient. If brushing is done frequently and thoroughly it can take the place of bathing plus stimulate new hair growth and prevent entanglement of hairs. Coats of some breeds are traditionally groomed with oils or other special liquids for promoting silkiness and ease of combing. Pet shops handle such products. Watch for wax in the ears, when a pup scratches and shakes its head from side to side, holding it to one side as it walks along. Impacted wax should come right out when you try to soften it with mineral or

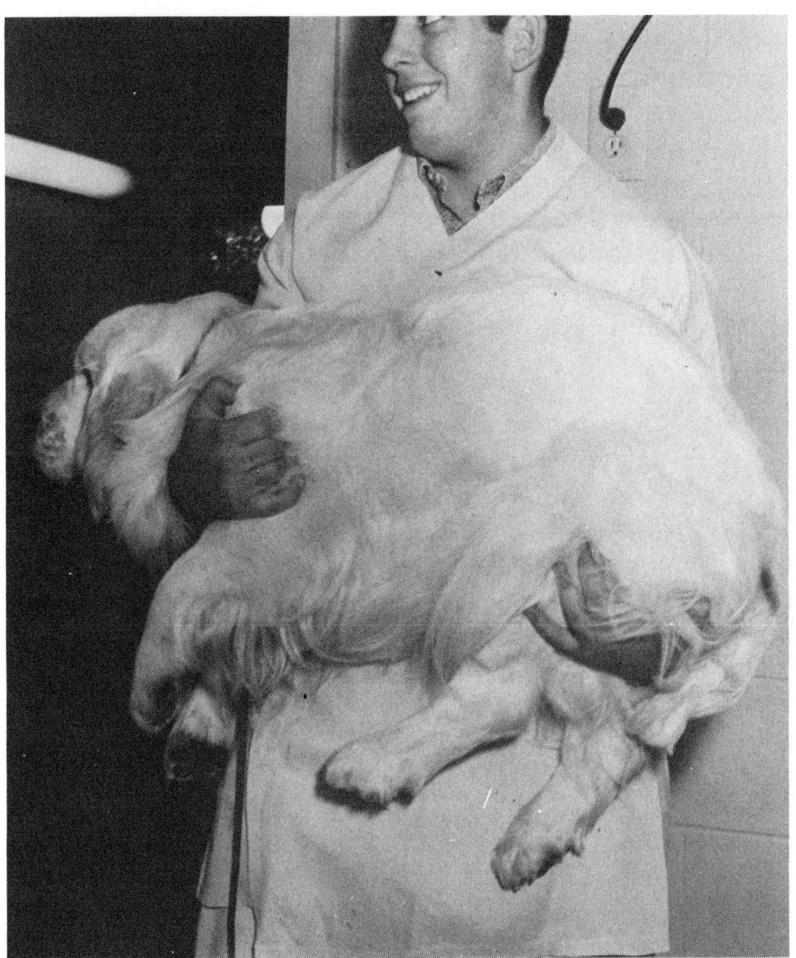

The forklift is the proper way to pick up a large dog, supporting its chest with one hand and using the other behind the back legs.

baby oil. If dirty ears continue to be a problem, consult your veterinarian as the problem could stem from earmites or other infectious agents.

IMMUNIZATION

Because some immunity to disease is generally transmitted with the antibodies contained in the colostrum (which precedes the first milk from the teat), veterinarians recommend immunization against distemper and hepatitis only after this immunity starts to wear off. This immunity begins to wane at about six to eight weeks; therefore, the puppies should receive their first distemper-hepatitis vaccination at six to eight weeks of age—failure to immunize the pups at this early age could result in early death. After this initial vaccination, your veterinarian will advise you when to return for additional injections for protection against distemper, hepatitis and leptospirosis. The rabies vaccine is generally not given until about 4 months of age but may vary depending upon

Puppies should be handled enough so that they become accustomed to it but not enough to spoil them. It is essential that puppies intended for the show ring tolerate all the handling required to position and groom them.

When the pups are ready for their own homes, the stud owner will take first choice.

the prevalence of the disease. Consult your veterinarian or public health authorities concerning regulations for rabies immunization.

PICK OF LITTER—A GENTLE REMINDER

Now, before you fall (more) in love with your bitch's new puppies, remember the pup destined to be the stud owner's choice. The stud owner has certainly not forgotten about it, even if you would like to forget. The stud owner will probably register your pup (the one he is getting) under his name as well as yours with his kennel club and the A.K.C. (American Kennel Club) pedigree records section.

Puppy socialization is an important aspect of creating an adult dog suitable for human companionship. And children are good puppy socializers, if they are taught to handle young dogs gently. Dogs with healthy temperaments usually respond positively to such handling. A genetically sound temperament in a dog should be a major consideration in any breeding program.

CHAPTER NINE

The X and Y of Breeding

A genetically perfect dog, at least for exhibition and kennel purposes, is free of diseases, defects and the "wrong" movements, but not including temperament.

Careful genetic planning before breeding may result in utterly confused litters without apparent rhyme or reason, while at other times, chance mating of two apparent zeros can produce extraordinary pups.

Genes, the basic building blocks of heredity, tend to be dominant or recessive in each generation, passing on through generation after generation of the "line" or breed which carries them. Some traits can be dominant in one breed but not in another; likewise with the recessive ones. Recessive genes can go into hiding, as it were, or are carried unnoted in "carriers," provided there are dominant genes to show up over these recessives. In time, once the dominant genes are absent, or stop "repressing" the recessive ones, as it were, the recessives can show up again in full force with their traits, good or bad, as the case may be.

THE GOOD MONK GREGOR

The laws of genetics, or heredity, were crystallized and stated by an Austrian Monk, Gregor Mendel, who worked with sweetpeas and other plants in his monastery garden. Certainly, breeding *results* had been observed for thousands of years before, but the good Monk Gregor patiently laid the basis of modern genetics by observing the mathematical probability of crossing strains. One of his experiments was as follows:

Cross two plants, one with round seed coats and one with wrinkled seed coats.
The first generation of plants from the above cross all had round seed coats, thus showing that round was dominant *over wrinkled.*
The second generation of plants produced from the above first-generation round seed coat plants showed three times as many round as wrinkled seed coats. Graphically demonstrated we have:

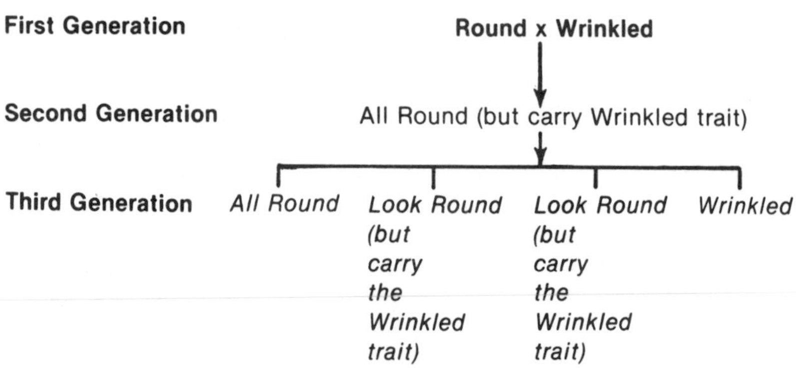

Of these three rounds and one wrinkled, the first kind (all round) will always produce round with other plants; the next two (look round, but carry wrinkled trait) will pass on the wrinkled trait as a recessive *trait (which will appear in later generations when no dominant round trait is present in the plants to which it will be crossed); the wrinkled kind will always produce wrinkled with no other plants as long as no dominant round trait is present to mask the wrinkled.*

If you read German, the original genetic insight given to the world appears in the *Verhandlungen naturforschender Verein in Brunn, Abhandlungen* IV, 1865 (but first published in 1866).

The Border Terrier is one of the oldest of the breed and was bred to be strictly a working Terrier, protecting stock that ranged far and wide from hill foxes that preyed on them.

Among America's most popular pointing breeds, the Brittany Spaniel, with an average weight of 35 pounds and a medium short coat that requires little grooming, is a favorite with apartment dwellers and huntsmen alike.

In Carl Muser's First Working Dog Club of America, organized in 1935, the Doberman Pinscher was trained to protect a child from kidnapping. Physical abuse to correct the dog did not enter into the training program. The tot's play pal now, could prove to be his rescuer later.

Now, what does that mean in relation to dogs? With any two dogs about to be mated, only six possibilities exist for what happens to a given trait (determined by two genes, one from each parent) according to Gregor Mendel's work (and all of modern science based upon it). Here are the six situations:

1. Each parent possesses a double dose, as it were, of the dominant gene. All progeny will be *purely dominant* for this trait, that is, will not carry the recessive gene.
2. Only one parent is pure for the dominant trait, as above in situation 1. The other appears to be pure, but is a carrier of the recessive gene. Fifty percent of the progeny will be pure, and 50% will appear to be pure, but are carriers of the recessive gene.
3. Only one parent appears to be purely dominant, but carries the recessive trait, that is, is *purely recessive. . .* it must be, otherwise it would look like the ones with a dominant gene (which masks the recessive one). That is, this purely recessive dog has a double dose of the recessive gene. Fifty percent of the pups will appear to be like the parent who is apparently dominant (but who really carries a recessive gene). Fifty percent will be like the purely recessive parent. That is, all the pups carry either one or two recessive genes for the trait in question.
4. Both parents appear to be purely dominant, but each carries one gene for recessive trait. The pups from this mating will be 25% purely dominant with both dominant genes, 50% apparently dominant like the parents (but carrying a recessive gene), and 25% look like one of the recessive grandparents from whom the parents obtained the recessive genes.
5. One parent is purely dominant (with two dominant genes). The other parent is purely recessive (with two recessive genes). All pups will look like the parent with the dominant trait, but each pup carries one recessive gene.
6. Both parents are purely recessive. All pups must be like them. Parents and pups all have a double dose of the recessive gene.

In general, if a pup has a trait which is not evident in either parent, then this trait results from a recessive gene. Two parents with dark eyes and nose, for example, who give rise to a puppy

Genes that would rob a field dog of an instinctive interest in birds apparently have not gained dominance in this eager Irish Setter.

with light eyes and nose means that the background of *both* parents includes dogs with the recessive genes for light eyes and nose. A mating of this pup with another dog with light eyes and light nose cannot produce a dog with dark eyes and dark nose, ever. Only when a dominant gene (for dark eyes and nose) is introduced will it "repress" the recessive gene in some of the pups and then show up.

Beware, however, of oversimplifying the transmission of traits. Genes may act in different ways, according to which ones occur together in one individual. Staffordshire fighting skill, bloodhound man-trailing, greyhound fleet footedness, as examples, are due to an intricate interaction of many genes or traits,

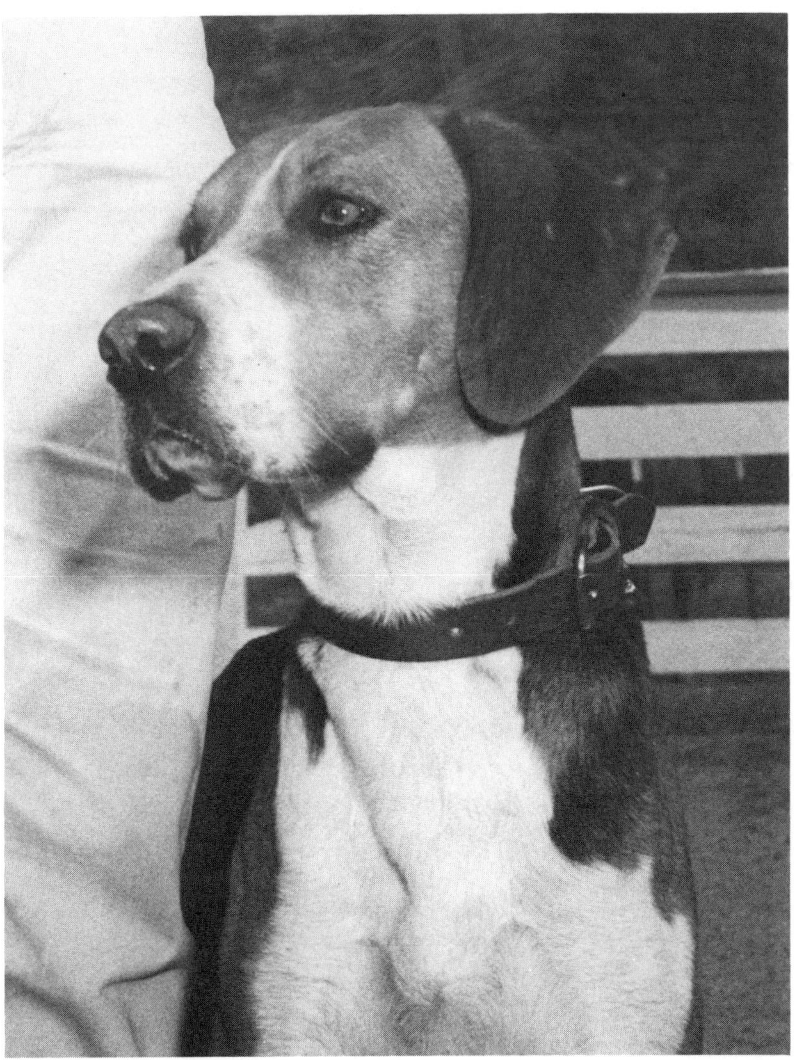

An instinct for the chase was one of the dominating factors that entered into the breeding program for this English Foxhound. Foxhounds, like Coonhounds, may not be penalized in conformation judging for scars, torn ears or the like incurred as they pursued the purpose for which they were bred.

not simple choices like round seed coat or wrinkled seed coat. At times the best you can do is to select the best individual of the best line or family exhibiting the trait(s) you want.

RECESSIVES AND DEFECTS

Most breeders are aware of the hazards associated with "inbreeding," or the close breeding of relatives. Inbreeding can amplify the problems associated with recessive genes and lead to genetic defects. Some of the commonly encountered defects which arise from inbreeding are:

Patella (knee cap) luxation.
Hair lip and cleft palate
Night blindness
Deafness
Hernia
Timidity, associated with gun shyness in certain breeds
Tendency to urinate when overly excited
Eye or retinal defects
Cataracts
Innumerable anatomical defects
Malocclusion (undershot or overshot jaws)
Hip dysplasia

Some recessive conditions which are not necessarily defects are:

Pearl eyes or yellow eyes (recessive to brown)
Dewclaws (recessive to no dewclaws)
Short hair (recessive to long hair)
Wire hair (recessive to smooth)
Coarse hair (recessive to fine)
Straight hair (recessive to curly)
Sparse (recessive to dense)
Drawling voice (recessive to chop voice)
No interest in birds (recessive to interest in birds)
No interest in water (recessive to going into the water)
Hunting in a straight line (recessive to quartering—a meander sort of hunting pattern)

And the list can go on much farther.

Recessive genes can come back from long ago. A Boxer can throw white puppies to remind us of the Bull Terrier in its

A pedigreed fawn Boxer bitch bred to a fawn stud may throw all-white puppies, reminiscent of the Bull Terrier in its history. Conscientious breeding attempts to cull undesirable traits. It's easy when the faults are caused by coupling of dominant genes. When recessives are responsible, it is more difficult to control.

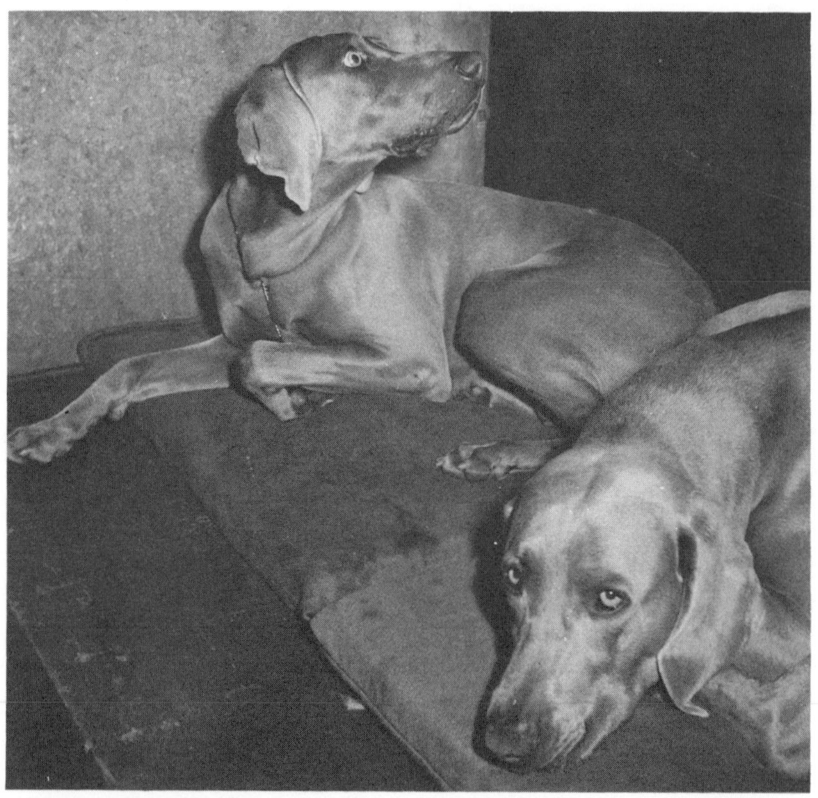

The silver gray coat of the Weimaraner, the only color accepted in its standard, was the result of pairing of recessive genes when this color mutation first occurred in the creation of the breed. Occasionally, a puppy will be thrown with long hair or black and tan markings, bespeaking the presence of these characteristics in the Weimaraner's ancestral breeds.

history. A Weimaraner can throw a long-coated puppy, recalling what other breeds were mated into the strain.

MUTATION AND SEX-LINKAGE

Despite "rules" of gene dominance and recessiveness, sudden surprises (mutations) can happen and continue on thereafter, breeding true, as the geneticist says, to mean that a newly appeared trait continues to pass on from generation to generation, at least to the next mutation which could change it.

Some characteristics are coupled—linked, as the geneticist says, to the sex of the individual. Lethal genes cause conditions incompatible with life, such as brain or heart defects which are very severe. Lethal genes are recessive, and if two dogs with recessive genes pass these on as a "double dose" to a puppy, then nature would somehow cull out that pup herself, and it would not survive. However, other puppies in the litter would still carry the recessive lethal gene.

Close relatives (brothers, sisters, mothers, fathers, sons, daughters) are interbred together only when dogs are faultless with the hope they are not carrying recessive, undesirable traits. This concentration of desired traits is good if we are certain that only desired traits are concentrated. Any deviate from the acceptable standard among the newborn pups are often culled—put to sleep—or better yet, altered, and given as a pet to a neighborhood child or family.

Relatives—including quite distant ones—are linebred. Linebreeding is somewhat like inbreeding in that the breeder does not (knowingly) add any new traits into the hereditary picture.

BREEDING TECHNIQUES

Crossbreeding joins two breeds for better or for worse; *outbreeding* (or outcrossing) joins two strains of one breed, thus allowing for improvement of traits which were fixed in a breed previously by *inbreeding* or close breeding of related individuals. *Linebreeding* consolidates and improves further on the desired traits concentrated by inbreeding. These concepts are discussed somewhat more below.

Unlike breeds are crossbred to create new breeds. The first generations produce mutts or mongrels until the new breed stabilizes (and finds a sponsoring kennel club!)

Unlike dogs from the same breed (but of different strains) are outbred or outcrossed to introduce a new trait, or to breed out a fault. Outbreeding is also defined as mating very distantly related or unrelated dogs; outcrossing is sometimes defined as mating dogs of unrelated inbred lines.

SELECTION

The rule is: desired traits are bred in and kept in, and faults are bred out. Faults caused by dominant genes are easy to spot and breed out of the strain. Faults due to recessive genes, however, are not apparent in dogs "masked" by the effects of the dominant genes. Pedigrees are therefore of value to spot these recessive genes in the background of the dogs concerned. But do not make the mistake of many breeders who look only at the pedigree on paper, and disregard completely the individual traits of the dogs being bred. It seems, luckily, that some things cannot just be reduced to paper, but must be perceived in the flesh, as it were. When mating two dogs, do not, of course, mate those that have the same faults if you wish to breed out these faults. If you wish to have only bi-color dogs, for example, do not mate two tri-color dogs together. Tri-color is recessive to bi-color, and if two dogs happen to be tricolor, that means that they have no dominance for bi-color, and the tri-color will always predominate in the offspring. This same thing goes with hair and coats; the same concept applies, of course, to other characteristics. Do not breed two albinos and expect anything but albinos. Do not breed two short-haired dogs and expect long-haired dogs; short hair is recessive to long hair, and as long as neither of the parents have the dominant genes for long-haired condition, the short hair will always be evident. If you breed two long-haired dogs together, then some of them will be long-haired and some may be short-haired, depending, of course, upon how many recessive genes they carry for short hair. There are some cases, also, in which you may get neither short hair nor long hair, but something in between; and this gets us into the intricacies of formal genetics, which we certainly do not want to get into here. There are many fine treatises on this subject; bibliographic references to these books may be obtained at your local library, from your veterinarian, or from a well-stocked pet shop.

BREEDING IN THE NEED FOR HUMAN HELP

Breeding has unfortunately led to unnatural (to say the least) breeds. Dogs of these "created" breeds would surely not survive

The Italian Greyhound, though it bears the name of the sight and racing hound believed to be its ancestral progenitor, has been bred for no functional purpose. It is intended primarily as a lap dog and companion. Some individuals of the breed have weighed as little as five pounds.

Origins of the Irish Wolfhound, dating back to written records of the second century, are clothed in folklore and romantic legend. Bred originally to run down wolves and the six-foot-tall Irish elk, they are rarely used for such purposes now, but are supposedly still at their best when pitted against the American timberwolf.

Hip dysplasia, a condition that frequently results from inbreeding too closely, afflicts many large breeds. In the case of working breeds and sporting breeds, the occurrence of hip dysplasia can cancel out the purposes for which they were bred.

indefinitely if their human owners did not stand by to help. To wit: broadheaded dogs (bulldogs) have whelping problems because heads do not always pass through the pelvis easily or at all. Dachshunds (half a dog high and a dog and a half long) commonly have disc problems. Pekingese and Pugs may have nasal and breathing problems.

MARKETING

Membership in a local kennel or breed club, in addition to the A.K.C., helps to sell your new litter. Assistance by a well known breeder is helpful. Advertising in dog publications and local newspapers is also an available outlet for selling a litter of pups. If you sell to dog lovers who do not wish to show the dog, but do

A pedigree tells you what your puppy has been bred for and what traits you may logically expect to appear. It is helpful also when you wish to breed the pup as a mature animal.

wish to give a new pet a good home, advise them on the good and bad points of the breed itself, if you want to. Do not burden the pet-seeker with esoteric breed standards; this could ruin the sale. Show, but do not overshow; do not confuse prospective buyers with too much choice. Almost *all* puppies are lovable.

It is unwise to accept returned "merchandise" because outside disease could gain entry to your kennel with the returnee. Perhaps your veterinarian could be the go-between. The new owner should be encouraged to get the puppy to the veterinarian within a short time of its purchase to get a clean bill of health for any defects or disease. If found defective, the puppy could then be returned immediately to you. Of course, there are some cases where no defect exists, except in the communication between family members of the pup's new owner (or would-be owner). In these cases the pup is not wanted at all, and the purchaser apologetically comes back with the creature in a cardboard box, tries not to look into the pup's eyes and tells you it was a mistake. I would first try to imbue the purchaser with the spirit to go home and try again. In the end, it is always best to take the pup back rather than let it face execution or abandonment, or worse yet, abuse or neglect in a home where it is not wanted. Try to assist the new owner with their problems, for there may be a simple solution that will allow both owner and pet to have the rewarding experience of loving and being loved.

ADMINISTRATIVE DETAILS

For information on the standard for your breed and how to register a new litter, pedigreed dog owners in most English-speaking countries may write to the following:

American Kennel Club
51 Madison Ave.
New York, N.Y. 10010

Australian National Kennel Club
Royal Show Grounds
Ascot Vale, Victoria
Australia

British Kennel Club
1 Clarges Street
Piccadilly, London W.1
England

Canadian Kennel Club
111 Eglinton Avenue East
Toronto 12, Ontario
Canada

Irish Kennel Club
4 Harcourt Street
Dublin 2
Ireland

New Zealand Kennel Club
P.O. Box 523
Wellington 1
New Zeland

AFTERWORD

What have you done for the breed? Have you raised the standard of the breed? Have you brought it closer to its ideal—the ideal standard being the theoretical peak of perfection?

The breed is bettered by improving on fertility, hardiness (or vigor), length of life and temperament. Hopefully each of your litters contributed to bringing out the best traits in the breed. Hopefully, too, you have acquired a feel for a good dog. . . regardless of what its papers say about it. Some people who work with animals seem able literally to *talk* the best out of their creatures. Perhaps you can develop such a rapport with dogs that refuse to mate, with bitches that need encouragement in whelping, with semi-conscious whelps as you give them artificial respiration and with all the little pups who need firm and loving care to start them off right as part of someone else's home. To many homes, the dog breeder is both Santa Claus and the stork. Do a good job!

Index